JET HARRIS

JET HARRIS

IN SPITE OF EVERYTHING

DAVE NICOLSON

MUSIC MENTOR BOOKS

York, England

British Library Cataloguing-in-Publication Data
A catalogue record for this book is available from the British Library.

ISBN-13: 978-0-9562679-2-4

Published worldwide by Music Mentor Books *(Proprietor: G.R. Groom-White)*
69 Station Rd, Upper Poppleton, York YO26 6PZ, North Yorkshire, England.
Telephone/Fax: +44 (0)1904 330308 *Email:* music.mentor@lineone.net

Cover design and photographs by Dave Nicolson.

Printed and bound in Great Britain by Impressions Print And Publish
www.printandpublish.co.uk

For Bruno

BOOKS BY DAVE NICOLSON

Biography

Bobby Thompson – A Private Audience

Interviews

On The Road
26 hitmakers of the Fifties and Sixties
tell their own amazing stories

On The Road Again
15 hitmakers of the Fifties
tell their own amazing stories

Back On The Road Again
14 hitmakers of the Fifties and Sixties
tell their own amazing stories

Acknowledgements

My thanks to: Margaret Harris, Janet Harris, Chris Tremlett, Mike Berry, the late Tommy Bruce, Clem Cattini, Billie Davis, Vince Eager, Royston Ellis, Brian Gregg, Cliff Hall, Wee Willie Harris, Frank Ifield, Laurel Jones, Roger LaVern, John Leyton, Brian 'Licorice' Locking, the late Tony Meehan, Alec Merrick, P.J. Proby, Cliff Richard and Bruce Welch.

I wish to thank my publisher, George White, for his enthusiasm and hard work, an excellent editing job, and for providing a necessary index. My appreciation is recorded to the 'Man With The Golden Arm' for his memorable music and everyone who very kindly loaned material from their own collections for the illustrations which enhance this book. Also, John Beecher (Rollercoaster Records), Gareth Jones and John Poole for useful supplementary information and research.

Thanks also to my son Peter for his generous technical support on the computer front, to Maureen for her willing assistance, and to Bill Sturrock for the loan of Shadows material.

This book is also dedicated to all those people whose lives were affected in any way by Jet Harris, both professionally and personally, and especially for Margaret Harris and her sons.

Finally, it is for the lives of Matthew Redpath and Jack Nicolaou, the happy memory of 'Mrs Wilson' and her family of Elswick, Newcastle upon Tyne.

SPECIAL THANKS TO

Jet Harris Fan Club (**www.jetharrisfanclub.co.uk**).

Billie Davis Fan Club (**www.billied.com**).

John Fisher, Recent & Rare Records, Unit 8, Bridge Court, 64 Bridge St, Evesham, Worcs WR11 4RY (Tel: 01386 422123, **www.recent.teg.co.uk**)

John Beecher, Rollercoaster Records (**www.rollercoasterrecords.com**). Copies of the *Inside Jet Harris* CD still available!

David Parker, *The Beat* magazine, Kingsley House, Home Close, Teffont, Salisbury, Wiltshire SP3 5QY (Tel: 01722 716268 or 716781, **www.kingsleyhousepublishers.com**). The best gig guide around.

Trevor Simpson, author of *Small Town Saturday Night.* Many more previously unpublished Shadows photographs appear in both volumes of this beautifully illustrated, full-colour celebration of Halifax's musical heritage. For more info see **www.smalltownsaturdaynight.co.uk**.

Contents

Introduction

My dealings with Jet spanned a number of years. Having given an interview for my book, *Back On The Road Again*, in 2004, he approached me after publication and asked me if I was man enough to write his autobiography. I did my 'homework' on Jet and responded with a question for him: would *he* be man enough to see a 'warts and all' account of his life in print? This took him aback, but eventually he elected to proceed.

Unfortunately, although I completed the manuscript, this venture foundered on several rocks. As a result, I removed all of Jet's interview material and proceeded to write the biography which you are now holding.

Readers will appreciate that the interviews in the second part of the book were all carried out during Jet's lifetime and I have therefore left them unaltered in the interests of accuracy.

Jet Harris's story is probably as familiar to the general public as it is to Shadows' fans. His show business tale of a fallen idol who enjoyed immense success, then suffered an equally great decline fuelled by alcohol, has been covered piecemeal in books and articles, as well as TV and newspaper interviews.

We didn't hear much about 'sex, drugs and rock'n'roll' in the late '50s and early '60s, but it existed. Initially, with his mean, moody look and blond quiff, Jet personified the Drifters/Shadows even more than the exciting lead guitar work of Hank B. Marvin. Teenage girls went for him in a big way and teenage boys felt that he was the kind of man you wanted to keep your girlfriend well away from. He had that natural dark edge and appearance of the little hard-case Teddy boy from down the street who you'd better not cross.

His loyal band of fans need no convincing that, above all else, he was a survivor and, like other artists who have suffered setbacks, illness and tragedy in their lives, they admired him even more because they could identify with him.

The purpose of this book is not only to mark Jet's life by documenting his career and contribution to UK pop music, but, more importantly, by using this compilation of interviews to provide a rare glimpse behind the public face. To find out what it was like to know, perform alongside, live with, love and suffer because Terry 'Jet' Harris's life was entwined with your own.

The people interviewed here cover nearly all of his life, from infancy to his eventual triumph over alcohol at the age of 57. On that journey there was much happiness, many tears and, it has to be said, an immense amount of damage to himself and others. Jet worked his way quickly through *three* successful pop careers (the Drifters/Shadows, Jet Harris solo artist, and Jet Harris & Tony Meehan) before suffering severe injuries in a road accident. Four marriages and several affairs were also racked up, and a number of children fathered.

Many people think that Jet simply squandered a great talent and golden opportunities that some artists can only dream of; that he was selfish, spoiled and reckless. Some blame his alcoholism – nowadays recognised as a medical condition, rather than a wilful act by the drinker; others may see it as a spiritual journey. His greatest achievement as an artist had to be his many chart successes, but as a man it was his courageous victory over alcohol which has to take pride of place.

Why did Jet have a propensity to drink? The study of alcohol dependency still has a long way to go, but whether it was his genetic inheritance, private and public pressures – or a combination of all of them – he and we will probably never know. What is certain, is that his alcoholism devastated his life and the lives of those who were closest to him. There is always a high price for survival and in Jet's life many people had to pay it.

In the final analysis, however, Jet Harris, MBE will be remembered for his achievements as a creative and trailblazing bass guitarist whose outstanding musicianship and influence will endure for years to come.

Dave Nicolson
March 2011

A Life

Kid Harris

By the summer of 1939, British optimism which followed the signing of the Anglo-German Agreement by Hitler and Chamberlain on 30 September 1938 counted for nothing. Hitler sneeringly referred to it as a 'scrap of paper'. If the 'Führer' hadn't been so obsessed with world domination, he would have had all the makings of a first-class agent and manager. In a surprise pact, Germany and Russia decided to carve up Poland, and Europe was divided and moving towards war. Anyway, before your eyes glaze over, that's the end of the history lesson. With these storm clouds overhead, Terence Harris was born on 6 July 1939 – two months before the declaration of World War II on 3 September – in the Honeypot Lane Maternity Ward, Kingsbury in London.

Terence was the only child of Winifred ('Wyn') Frances (*née* Terry) and William Harris. Bill was employed as a press tool setter with United Dairies at Park Royal. In between keeping house and looking after her youngster, Wyn worked variously as a telephone operator, typesetter and proofreader. His father was an orphan, but there were plenty of aunties and uncles on his mother's side, and in spite of the wartime bombing of London young Terry seems to have enjoyed a solid family life.

As he worked in a 'reserved occupation', Bill was not called up for military service, so the young lad had the added stability – denied to many children at that time – of two parents at home during his formative years, as well as his extended family. Through his father, he acquired a knowledge and lifelong interest in the natural world. For anyone growing up at this time there was the terror and panic of the bombings and air raid sirens, but in the post-war years bomb sites made great adventure playgrounds for kids, plus there was the magic of radio and going to 'the pictures'.

At five years of age, Terry started his education at St Mary's School, progressing to Dudden Hill Secondary Modern and later Willesden Technical College.

His musical awakening took place around the time he passed a scholarship for Willesden Tech. Here, he developed an interest in jazz and started taking clarinet lessons at the age of 13. In those days, his idols included jazz greats like Oscar Peterson, Charlie Parker and Ella Fitzgerald, though he was particularly inspired by pianist Winifred Atwell (or, more specifically, her left hand when she played boogie) and bassist Percy Heath of the Modern Jazz Quartet.

Around the same time, he also started to excel in athletics and games – football in particular – and was dubbed 'Jet' by his classmates because of his speed as a sprinter.

Music and all that jazz

In the early 1950s, popular British music was made up in the main of domestic and US dance bands, harmony-style groups and solo singers. Britain was fronting the likes of David Whitfield, Frankie Vaughan, Jimmy Young and Petula Clark, while our American cousins had Frank Sinatra, Eddie Fisher, Johnnie Ray, Frankie Laine, Tennessee Ernie Ford and Guy Mitchell. The Billy Cotton and Cyril Stapleton bands and their featured vocalists were part of our radio music fabric.

The Brits had a fight on their hands, as youngsters in the post-war austerity of Britain had fallen in love with nearly all things American. Blame the glamour imagery of the movies, bubblegum, American comics and the influence of the Yanks being stationed over here during the war. The Grade Organisation and other promoters started to bring over top-line American acts for stints at the London Palladium followed by nationwide tours.

Jazz music had enjoyed a strong following in this country from the 1920s, particularly among the upper classes, who embraced it without prejudice as to the colour of the musician's skin. Duke Ellington headlined the London Palladium, the premier theatre in the world, as far back as 1933. For the new generation of rebellious young people of all classes, jazz offered an exciting and fun alternative to the sentimental ballads and dance bands favoured by their parents, which seemed to have been around forever. After all, it's pretty hard to be a James Dean – with or without a cause – if you're listening to the 'Wakey-wakey!' shouts of Billy Cotton or *Family Favourites* over Sunday lunch.

Jet had switched to double bass when he discovered he couldn't play boogie on the clarinet. While still at Willesden Tech, he began frequenting the capital's jazz clubs and immersing himself in the music. His favourite hangout was the Mapleton Club near Leicester Square, which is also where he played his first paid gig – on double bass – with four of his college pals as 'The Delinquents'. Along the way Jet also became acquainted with jazz bassist Sammy Stokes, who gave him lessons on technique in exchange for cigarettes.

After leaving the Tech at the age of 15, Jet started an apprenticeship as a sheet metal worker at United Dairies, where his father was still employed.

Meanwhile, skiffle music exploded onto the UK music scene. Skiffle was a kind of home-made folk music derived from the jazz and blues of the 1920s and '30s, and particularly the versions played by poor blacks and whites in both country and city. Having to make their own entertainment very often meant using improvised makeshift instruments for effect and fun. Everything from boxes and combs to bottles and jugs were put to good and ingenious use.

Some of the early songs given the UK skiffle treatment by professional musicians like Lonnie Donegan were established folk-blues songs like Leadbelly's 'Rock Island Line' and 'John Henry'. Even if the sight of Beryl Bryden playing washboard was unforgettable, these songs were usually performed by professional musicians using professional instruments with some improvised ones employed for novelty effect. Donegan was the king of UK skiffle having started as part of Chris Barber's Jazz Band, where he was given a featured solo spot for such music.

Over the next couple of years skiffle thrust its way into the general public's consciousness with some catchy hits which seemed so simple to reproduce. Importantly for the British music scene, however, many teenagers, armed with mother's washboard and thimble, and home-made basses (constructed from tea chests, a broom shank and string) were moved to become performers themselves and emulate the likes of Lonnie Donegan, the Vipers, Chas McDevitt, Bob Cort *et al*, all of whom enjoyed considerable success.

A thriving culture of coffee bars in and around London provided a good home for skiffle before it later hit the theatres and variety tours, and it was the place to be for anyone who wanted to be in on the action. Small wonder, then, that Jet packed in his apprenticeship after a year and took a job behind the counter at the 2I's coffee bar in Soho's Old Compton Street.

The 2I's had been opened in April 1956 by a couple of Australian wrestlers – Paul Lincoln (*aka* the mask-wearing 'Dr Death') and 'Rebel' Ray Hunter, who named their establishment after the building's owners, two brothers called Irani. The coffee bar's major attraction was the cellar (or 'Black Hole of Calcutta' as it quickly became known), which featured live music. The Vipers, who became one of the leading skiffle groups in the country, started playing there in July 1956, attracting crowds of customers as well as many other aspiring musicians.

Quickly, the 2I's acquired a reputation as a breeding ground for new talent. The 'do-it-yourself' nature of skiffle made it easy for visitors to sit in with whoever was playing that day, and Jet would often go downstairs after work to watch or participate.

Seeing their only child move out of his home to pursue what was – and still is – a very uncertain career must have worried Bill and Wyn tremendously, but there is no evidence that they did not support their son in his musical aspirations. What the teenager himself made of it all one can only imagine, but Soho's rich mix of characters, both artistic and shady, must have been heady stuff for a young lad brought up in a conventional and nurturing household. If he hadn't lost his virginity by this point, he would now have very little excuse for not doing so. Britain itself may have been a few years away from the so-called Swinging Sixties, but the capital had always been years ahead for trends in both fashion and morality.

Rockin' and rollin'

Skiffle music and rock'n'roll may have both burst upon the UK music scene in the same year of 1956, but skiffle quickly began fighting for oxygen. Elvis, Little Richard, Chuck Berry, Fats Domino, Pat Boone (before he was decried as a crooner who profited from the hits of black artists), the Platters and Frankie Lymon & The Teenagers led an irresistible charge. Never at a loss, Britain threw up to the battlements home-grown rockers like Tommy Steele, Terry Dene and the energetic piano-pounder, Wee Willie Harris.

When not wrestling, Paul Lincoln also managed Terry Dene and Wee Willie, and it was he who offered the young Jet his first professional job, as bass player in Terry Dene's backing group, the Dene Aces. (A few years later, Jet revealed that the engagement had first been offered to his mentor, Sammy Stokes, who turned it down and recommended Jet for it, to give him the experience.)

Dene had enjoyed two Top 20 hits that summer with 'A White Sport Coat' and 'Start Movin'' and had been booked to headline a national tour. Jet duly made his professional debut in Middlesbrough in the autumn of 1957. However, there was a big disappointment in store. After a couple of weeks, Lincoln took him to one side and gently broke it to him that he wasn't yet good enough.

So, for Jet it was back to learning his notes and honing his skills in Soho by practising hard and taking the opportunity to play with whoever was around in a scene that was gathering momentum every day. His application was rewarded when he got gigs backing singer Larry Page ('The Teenage Rage') and with the bandleader from *6.5 Special,* Don Lang.

However, his real breakthrough came when Paul Lincoln sent him out on a theatre tour as bassist with Tony Crombie & His Rockets. Titled *Rockin' At The 21's*, the show also featured Les Hobeaux, the Most Brothers and headliner Wee Willie Harris, and toured for 22 weeks in late 1957 and early 1958. Crombie's group had their own spot, as well as providing backing for Wee Willie. On that tour Jet also acquired Mickie Most's pet monkey, Mosty.

That hair.

These were the dying days of variety theatre, and at some venues the bills were bizarre mixtures of rock'n'rollers, dancing troupes, acrobats, ventriloquists and performing animal acts.

Some of the old pros grudgingly admitted (years after, mind) that rock'n'roll acts extended the life of variety – traditionally entertainment for the whole family, whereas the strip shows and nude revues were instrumental in killing it off. In truth, once commercial television arrived in the mid-Fifties, with its heavy emphasis on popular entertainment, the bell was tolling loudly.

Up to this point in his career, Jet had only ever played the double bass. Shortly after the tour ended, Tony Crombie introduced him to a 'new invention' he had spotted in a Charing Cross Road music shop: the four-string electric bass guitar. It is unlikely that Jet was the first musician in the UK to play a bass guitar, but he became the most prominent and stylistically important. In his hands, the 'new' instrument aroused a great deal of interest and job offers began to increase.

He was invited by Wally Whyton to join the Vipers, by now an established and well-respected skiffle group, but struggling to hold their own against rock'n'roll.

Jet moved into their Eccleston Square basement flat in Victoria, which they shared with a menagerie of small animals including a fox and a skunk. Even little Mosty benefited, as Vipers' members John Pilgrim and Johnny Booker also had monkeys (Elvis and 'Iggins respectively) as pets.

According to pop legend, it was also the Vipers who first came up with the idea of bleaching Jet's hair – though former Les Hobeaux bassist Brian Gregg tells a different story *(see page 111)*!

During the summer of 1958, the group went into EMI's Abbey Road studio to cut half a dozen tracks with producer George Martin. 'Liverpool Blues' and 'Summertime Blues' were released as a single, but flopped. (The other four – 'The Fly', 'Banks Of The Ohio', 'Worried Man Blues' and 'Trouble In Mind' – stayed in the can until 1996, when they appeared on the Bear Family 3-CD compilation, *10,000 Years Ago*.)

By this time, skiffle was well and truly on its way out, and Jet could see the writing on the wall. He jumped ship soon after and got a job backing the Most Brothers on an October tour headlined by the Kalin Twins from the USA. As it turned out, it was to present him with the biggest break of his career.

Britain's latest teenage star

On the strength of their summer chart-topper, 'When', the American duo were brought over to Britain by the Grades to top a variety bill at London's Prince of Wales Theatre for two weeks, before embarking on a string of one-nighters for promoter Arthur Howes. The tour kicked-off on 5 October 1958 at the Victoria Theatre in Hanley and finished on 19 October at Colston Hall in Bristol. In between, it played Blackpool, Wigan, Glasgow, Manchester, Liverpool, Leicester, Sheffield, Newcastle upon Tyne, Birmingham and York.

The programme and running order were both on traditional variety theatre lines. Opening the show were the Londonairs ('The Men of Rhythm'), a trio consisting of guitar, accordion and double bass. They were followed by MC Tony Marsh, then the Most Brothers (also Jet's spot, albeit in the background), then Tony Marsh again, before *'Guest Star'* Eddie Calvert ('The Man With The Golden Trumpet') closed the first half.

Tony Marsh opened the second half and then introduced *'Britain's latest teenage star'*, Cliff Richard, with his group, the Drifters. After Cliff's spot, it was Tony Marsh again (they got their money's worth out of him!), followed by the Kalin Twins.

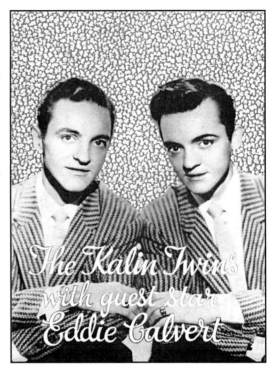

Cliff Richard started life as Harry Rodger Webb on 14 October 1940 in Lucknow, India, the only son of Rodger and Dorothy Webb (*née* Dazely). Three sisters followed: Donella ('Donna'), Jacqueline and Joan.

Seriously unsettled by the effects of partitioning in 1947, the Webbs left India and moved to England in 1948, arriving one month before Harry's eighth birthday. After staying with relatives in single-room accommodation in Carshalton and Waltham Cross, they obtained a council house at 12 Hargreaves Close in Cheshunt, Hertfordshire.

Harry, like thousands of other teenagers, was interested in the rock'n'roll music of Elvis Presley, Bill Haley, Little Richard, etc when it came along in 1956, and wanted to be a star himself. Norman Mitham, a school friend and neighbour, was also an early convert to the new music. In 1956, Harry joined a school vocal group called the Quintones. Around this time, his dad bought him a second-hand guitar and taught him the basic chords.

Leaving school with one GCE 'O' Level in English, young Harry had a couple of jobs including that of a credit control clerk at Atlas Lamps where Rodger worked. But his interests lay more and more with music. Skiffle was a big craze during 1956 and 1957. Harry joined the Dick Teague Skiffle Group in September

1957, where he met drummer Terry Smart.

Having decided that it was rock'n'roll for them, Harry and Terry broke away, and with guitarist Norman Mitham formed their own group, the Drifters, playing local clubs and pubs like the Five Horseshoes. It was at this pub that the Drifters were spotted by John Foster, a sewage worker. He asked them if they wanted to play at the 2I's coffee bar in Soho. The 2I's was already renowned for fuelling the careers of Tommy Steele and Terry Dene. Foster arranged an afternoon audition and, having passed it, the Drifters went back to play that evening. In the audience that night was future Drifter Bruce Welch, who went away impressed.

A one-week engagement followed, during which Ian 'Sammy' Samwell, on leave from the RAF, caught the show. Both Harry and Norman played rhythm guitar, but there was no lead guitar – cue Ian, who successfully auditioned and joined the group. It was at this point that Harry Webb became Cliff Richard following the offer of a gig in Ripley, Derbyshire. Promoter Harry Greatorex wanted a *named singer* and group, and not just a collective group name. So on Saturday night, 3 May 1958 Cliff Richard & The Drifters debuted.

Very quickly Norman Mitham became the group's first casualty as, with Cliff singing and playing rhythm guitar and Ian on lead, he was superfluous. Cliff and the boys made a demo record in an Oxford Street studio performing 'Lawdy Miss Clawdy' and 'Breathless'. Although they were not competitors, they made a 'starring' appearance at the Gaumont Theatre, Shepherds Bush on a Carroll Levis *Discoveries* show. The group went down a storm and Foster, trying to use the venue as a showcase for agents, enginereed further appearances. At one of these, George Ganjou, a former variety artist with the top-line adagio act, the Ganjou Brothers & Juanita, witnessed Cliff & The Drifters.

Impressed, Ganjou took the demo to EMI producer Norrie Paramor, who a few weeks later arranged an audition. Having passed the audition, a recording session was scheduled for a few weeks later. In the interim, Ian Samwell composed a song called 'Move It', which they took with them to the EMI session. It was handed to Paramor, who had selected only one song, 'Schoolboy Crush' (provided by Aberbach Music's Franklyn Boyd). Unsure of the band's musical abilities, Paramor had sessionmen Ernie Shear (guitar) and Frank Clarke (double bass) on hand. It was agreed that Ian would play rhythm guitar and Ernie lead guitar on 'Move It', which only took a couple of takes. Its release date was set for 29 August 1958 with 'Schoolboy Crush' as the 'A' side.

Having signed with George Ganjou as their agent, Cliff and the band were smartly booked into Butlin's holiday camp at Clacton-on-Sea for a month, where an advanced pressing of their first recordings got an airing. EMI also got the record onto Radio Luxembourg who plumped for 'Move It', which entered the charts on 12 September 1958 at No.28.

The record's success led to the booking for Cliff & The Drifters by promoter Arthur Howes on his October 1958 Kalin Twins UK tour. By then, Ian Samwell had moved onto bass and another guitarist, Ken Pavey, whom they had met at Butlins, had taken over on lead guitar. Unfortunately for Ken, he was not available for the Kalins tour, so manager John Foster went in search of a lead guitarist. Having failed to locate his first choice, Tony Sheridan, he was eventually pointed to Hank B. Marvin. Marvin agreed to the tour offer but insisted that his mate Bruce Welch should also be hired. So when they kicked off the tour the line up was Hank B. Marvin (lead guitar), Bruce Welch (rhythm guitar), Ian Samwell (double bass) and Terry Smart (drums).

The two Geordie schoolmates, Hank (Brian Rankin) and Bruce (Cripps), who met at Rutherford Grammar School in Newcastle upon Tyne had started off in different skiffle groups. Bruce's group was the Railroaders and Hank's was the Riverside Skiffle Group, and then the Crescent City Skiffle Group. Hank played banjo at the outset, but later forsook it for guitar. Both had success in and around Newastle as members of the Railroaders and earned regular money in working mens' clubs and social clubs.

In late 1957 they entered themselves for a talent contest at the Edmonton Granada, London and eventually earned a place in the finals held in April 1958. They finished in third place but,

Cliff Richard, 1958.

having already left school earlier in the year, decided to remain in the capital (their trips to London had made them more unsettled with life back home).

In the run-up, they met Pete Chester, son of comedian Charlie Chester, who led fellow contestants the Chesternuts. After the competition, Hank and Bruce joined the group and performed with them a few times.

The Chesternuts were spotted by impresario Leslie Conn, who paid for them to make a demo record which found its way onto a Columbia Records release – 'Teenage Love' *b/w* 'Jean Dorothy' – credited to the Five Chesternuts. This in turn led to an appearance on BBC TV's *6.5 Special*, where Charlie Chester introduced them. Not long after, the Chesternuts split up, so Hank and Bruce ('the Geordie Boys', as they were becoming known), headed for the 2I's and other Soho clubs hoping to play for pay and progress. It was here that they ran into Jet Harris, who had already impressed the Soho scene with his musical ability.

On one of the few occasions that Hank, Bruce and Jet took to the 2I's stage together, they were approached by 15-year-old drummer, Tony Meehan, who asked if he could join in. And so, unknown to any of them, one of the UK's most famous groups had been previewed. Tony, somewhat of a child prodigy and still a schoolboy, had been spotted early and invited to join the Worried Men, Adam Faith's ex-backing group.

Having made his entrance, he joined the group merry-go-round that prevailed at the time – with the most money being the deciding loyalty factor. Tony did stints with Vince Eager before forming the Playboys to back Vince Taylor. After this, he was asked to join the Vipers by Johnny Booker.

That September, Hank joined Jet and Tony on tour in the new Vipers, but quit after a week and returned to London. In *The Shadows by Themselves* Tony recalled Jet, who at that time was known as the 'Suede Kid' because of his clothes: 'He was a very quiet person, moody and often depressed.'

As luck would have it, by the time the tour started the Kalins' 'When' was on the wane and 'Move It', with Cliff's exciting vocal and Ernie Shear's excellent guitar work, was steadily climbing the charts. Its significance was not fully appreciated then, but many music experts have since come to regard 'Move It' as one of the classic British rock'n'roll records, and probably the only one that could hold its head up in American company at that time.

Cliff & his Drifters had been allocated the show's penultimate spot before the Kalin Twins, and such was his rapidly growing popularity and the clamour of audiences that Herbie and Hal Kalin could barely follow him. They asked for Cliff to close the first half, but Cliff and his management refused. The publicity of being Britain's new singing sensation and effectively stealing the show night after night from an American headline act was just too good to surrender.

Early on in the tour, Jet was approached by Cliff, who asked him if he would like to work for him. The singer was on the lookout for a better bass player than Ian Samwell, and Jet's hard-driving playing style was exactly what he wanted. Jet initially turned down the offer, but when he saw the rapturous reception Cliff received night after night, he quickly changed his mind.

Group changes weren't the only products of the Kalins engagement, as the inexperienced John Foster, who was by now getting out of his depth, found himself replaced by Franklyn Boyd as Cliff's business manager. Foster was retained for a while as Cliff's personal manager on a wage of £12 per week.

Drifting into the Shadows

A few weeks after the end of the tour, Jet made his TV debut backing Cliff on ABC TV's popular *Oh Boy!* and in the closing months of 1958 made a number of appearances on the show. By the end of the year Cliff was a nationally-known teen idol, mobbed by adoring female fans wherever he went.

However, his new bass player quickly became an attraction in his own right. With his blond, quiffed hair and dangerous, edgy look, Jet stood out from the three ordinary-looking guys who were his companions in Cliff's backing group. Very quickly he became a female fan magnet himself, providing a stark onstage contrast to the dark-haired romantic glamour of Cliff.

But Jet had now also reached the age of 19, and for him, as for thousands of other young men past their 18th birthday (tragically so in the case of Terry Dene), the spectre of military conscription – and with it the automatic loss of his music career – loomed. Fortunately for him, he failed the medical. Being declared 'Unfit For Service' meant he was free to pursue his life in show business.

The first Cliff & The Drifters recordings he played on were 'Livin' Lovin' Doll' and 'Mean Streak', cut in November 1958 for release in the New Year. Shortly after the session, drummer Terry Smart was replaced by 15-year-old Tony Meehan, who would contribute a great deal to shaping the group's future sound and popularity.

Hank, Bruce, Tony and Jet – now regarded by many as the classic Drifters/Shadows line-up – made their stage debut with Cliff at the Free Trade Hall, Manchester in January 1959.

Also that month, Franklyn Boyd's tenure as manager was terminated. After a three-week booking for Cliff & The Drifters at Finsbury Park Empire, which overlapped with Cliff's filming commitments for his first movie, *Serious Charge*, Cliff was so exhausted that Rodger Webb decided that he had to make changes. Desperately he cast around for advice from experienced people. One of these was Ray Mackender, an insurance underwriter and part-time deejay, who later managed Mark Wynter. Ray had become a friend of both Cliff and his parents

The Drifters.
Left to right: Jet Harris, Bruce Welch, Tony Meehan and Hank B. Marvin.

having met them at a 1958 party hosted by *Oh Boy!* organist Cherry Wainer. As a result of his deliberations and talks, Rodger fired Boyd by letter – and did the same to John Foster a few weeks later.   Rodger chose former jazz accordionist turned showbiz manager Tito Burns to handle his son's affairs – at least, until he was 21 – while agent Ganjou continued to draw his ten per cent.

In February, Cliff & The Drifters recorded a live session at EMI's Abbey Road studios in front of three hundred Cliff Richard fan club members which became his first LP, *Cliff*, released in April.

However, the Drifters were also keen to record in their own right, and with Cliff's encouragement and the support of producer/arranger Norrie Paramor, they were signed by EMI on 5 February 1959. For their debut single they recorded two vocal numbers, 'Feelin' Fine' and 'Don't Be A Fool With Love', which EMI also leased to Capitol for US release. Disappointingly, the record failed to connect on either side of the Atlantic, but at least they were on their way.

Their first instrumental, 'Chinchilla', appeared in May on Cliff's *Serious Charge* EP. This was followed by two more in June, 'Jet Black' and 'Driftin'' (composed by Jet and Hank respectively), on their second single. Unusually, the featured lead instrument on 'Jet Black' was Jet's electric bass guitar, giving the recording a novel sound, but it failed to sell.

This record too was scheduled for US release, but there was a problem. Unknown to Cliff and the Drifters (and presumably EMI management), several years earlier manager George Treadwell had copyrighted the 'Drifters' name in the USA, and now handled a very successful singing group by that name. When the Drifters' first Capitol release came to his attention, Treadwell took out an injunction and the single was withdrawn from sale. For the US issue of 'Jet Black', the group was hurriedly rechristened 'The Four Jets', though the shortcomings of the name quickly became apparent – after all, there was only one Jet. Sadly, the competition proved too strong and 'Jet Black' went the way of its predecessor, 'Feelin' Fine'.

Despite these initial disappointments, life must have been pretty good for these four young men. They were backing the country's hottest solo act, as well as developing their own identity and career. If touring in old buses and vans wasn't glamorous, then the groupies on offer at each venue must have been a compensation. Although the big money must have seemed a long way off (they were still receiving a straight salary at the time), the Drifters had made the scene and were nationally known.

Meanwhile, Cliff's career was continuing apace. In June 1959, he was honoured with a place on the *Royal Variety Performance*, held that year at the Palace Theatre, Manchester. Jack Good introduced Cliff, Marty Wilde, the Vernons Girls, the Dallas Boys and Lord Rockingham's XI in a special *Oh Boy!* segment. The rest of the show was taken up by representatives of the 'old guard': Liberace, Tommy Trinder, Anne Shelton, Arthur Askey, Ronnie Hilton, Jill Day and Russ Conway. Old-style variety was still alive and well when it came to royal shows and televised family entertainment.

That summer, Cliff enjoyed the biggest seller of that year with his fifth single, 'Living Doll'. A real career-maker for him, it was his first UK No.1 and also his first US hit, reaching No.30 in the *Billboard* 'Hot 100'.

Around this time, the Drifters began an interesting but now little-remembered association with the British beat poet, Royston Ellis. A teenager himself, Ellis wrote poetry about teenagers, for teenagers, and was concerned that it should reach its intended audience.

'I wanted teenagers to read, or at least hear, those poems. That was practically impossible, as young people hardly cared about reading newspapers, let alone poetry. I decided I needed to promote my poetry properly, like a pop star, if I wanted to reach teenagers. Cliff Richard was the pop idol of the moment and I resolved to discuss how to do that with him.'

The Webbs' friend, Ray Mackender, arranged for Ellis to meet Cliff at Radio Luxembourg's London studio:

'I can't say it was love at first sight, as Cliff was rather wary about the bearded, unwashed beatnik who gatecrashed the broadcast. However, Jet Harris, the bass guitarist of the then-Drifters, and himself something of a beat, had no such hesitation.

'He, Tony Meehan and I became firm friends. This friendship led to me developing the idea of performing my poems to music, so that I could bring them to the notice of the teenagers I was writing about. With Cliff's approval, the Drifters played backing while I read poems on television and stage shows.'

Ellis went on to write or co-write the first-ever books on Cliff (*Driftin' with Cliff Richard*), the Shadows (*The Shadows by Themselves*) and the British rock'n'roll scene (*The Big Beat Scene*) before leaving the UK in 1961 to explore the world and become a successful novelist, biographer and travel writer.

In October, Cliff and the Drifters travelled abroad for the first time to undertake a promotional tour of West Germany and Scandinavia. On the eve of their departure, Tony Meehan collapsed after their show at Cheshunt and was rushed to hospital with acute appendicitis. After a frantic search for a drummer who was not only good enough, but who also had a passport and was free to travel, Laurie Jay (later with Nero & The Gladiators) was quickly drafted in as a replacement.

Some time during October 1959, the Drifters became the Shadows (a UK tour poster for a 12 October appearance billed them as 'The Drifters', but these were usually printed weeks in advance). However, Cliff's 'Travellin' Light', also released that month, credits 'The Shadows'. What was clear, is that after their earlier problems with US record releases they needed to come up with a new name for home and abroad use to avoid future difficulties. In the course of a two-man brainstorming session conducted by Hank and Jet over a drink at the Six Bells pub near Ruislip, Jet came up with 'the Shadows' and when it was put to Bruce and Tony it was immediately agreed. (Thankfully, no one was aware that at the time US singer Bobby Vee's backing group was also called 'The Shadows'! Any potential problem vanished when Vee's band disbanded within a short time.)

The Shadows also made their screen debut that December, playing Cliff's backing group in his second movie, *Expresso Bongo*. That same month, they released their first record under their new name, 'Saturday Dance' *b/w* 'Lonesome Fella'. Again it did nothing – three releases and three misses. No matter, 1959 had been a great year for Cliff and the boys – even if his new manager, Tito Burns, only had his sights set on developing the singer's career. In *Cliff Richard, The Bachelor Boy* Hank Marvin confirmed that 'Tito Burns never managed the Shadows. He managed Cliff, and Cliff employed the Shadows.'

Oh, Carol

1959 was also a pivotal year for Jet on a personal level. He had met Carol Costa in late 1958, when she and her sisters came to see Cliff and the Drifters at the Chiswick Empire. After a brief courtship, they were married on 13 June 1959 at St Paul's Church, Hounslow Heath. About a thousand fans turned up for the wedding, but Cliff and Tony Meehan weren't there as they had gone off on holiday to Italy with Cliff's friend Ronnie Ernstone and a girl named Pam.

19 59... Marriage solemnized at S. Paul's Church

of S. Paul Thornbury Heath in the County of Middlesex in the Parish

No.	When married	Name and surname	Age	Condition	Rank or profession	Residence at the time of marriage	Father's name and surname	Rank or profession of father
224	June 13 1959	Terence Harris	19	Bachelor	Insurance	40 Wentworth Villas Willesdon NW10	Leslie Ian Harris	Registrar seller
		Carol Ann Costa	17	Spinster	—	3 Cedar Rd	Carl Aubrey William Costa	Chartered Accountant institution

Married in the church according to the rites and ceremonies of the Church of England, or after — by me,

This marriage was solemnized between us, { T. Harris / Ca. Costa }

In the presence of us, { W. Harris / C.R.W. Costa }

J.P. Bolton Vicar

30

Much has been written – particularly in newspaper interviews with Jet and Carol over the years – about the break-up of their marriage and Cliff's affair with Carol. Cliff has spoken about it in the Steve Turner biographies, which also described the clandestine way in which it was conducted. In *Cliff Richard, The Bachelor Boy*, Carol revealed that her affair with Cliff was consummated when he visited her at the Ealing flat of a friend, Vicky Marshall, with whom she was staying at the time.

How much the Shadows knew about what was going on is debatable, but in *Cliff: An Intimate Portrait of a Living Legend*, the authors mention one occasion when, following a Blackpool concert Tony Meehan was going to share a sleeper to London with Cliff, but gave up his berth to Carol.

Bruce Welch and Tony Meehan have since both expressed the view that it was Carol who did the chasing, but Cliff was clearly not an unwilling victim. As he conceded in a 1993 *South Bank Show* special: 'She fell in love with me and I loved her. She reminded me of Brigitte Bardot, who I had a thing about.'

Carol, who was also interviewed for the programme, added, 'When you're together and there's a strong physical attraction, it's difficult not to make love. In the end we did... Cliff was a virgin.'

The ongoing debate about Cliff's sexuality and celibate lifestyle – to say nothing of the only known instance of his sexual intercourse with a female – have continued to fascinate the public, providing the newspapers with an endlessly recyclable story (and Jet and Carol with an occasional source of extra income). As recently as 13 December 2008, the *Daily Mail* ran a double-page spread based on an interview with Jet titled CLIFF RICHARD STOLE MY WIFE, while on 19 September 2009 the same paper devoted two pages to Carol's revelations under the headline HOW CLIFF SEDUCED ME IN MY CURLERS.

The story appears to be that of a simple love triangle, but in reality Jet and Carol's marriage hit the rocks very quickly, and their relationship became stormy and physically violent. Cliff has stated that Jet was drunk a lot of the time, and was not a good drunk. The Shadows witnessed the violence too. In Steve

Carol in 1964.

Turner's *Cliff Richard The Biography*, Tony Meehan recalled one occasion when he was forced to drag Jet off Carol because he had her pinned to the floor and was punching her. By all accounts Carol was a feisty woman who could give as good as she got, but clearly things were degenerating rapidly.

It must have been a particularly difficult time for Jet. Seeing his marriage fall apart would have been hard enough, but carrying on in the knowledge that his boss was involved with his wife – and being unable to do anything about it without blowing his career to pieces – must have been unbearable. Small wonder then, that he turned to the bottle for solace. If there was a point when the normal drinking of a young man began to head towards dependency, this was it.

In December 1959, Cliff & The Shadows appeared in the pantomime, *Babes In The Wood*, at the Globe Theatre, Stockton-on-Tees. Carol, now heavily pregnant, accompanied her husband. While driving in Stockton, Jet was responsible for a serious collision with an oncoming car which left him with a broken collarbone, Carol with broken ribs and a fractured skull, and other passengers with a variety of minor injuries. He was charged with dangerous driving and related offences.

Over the years Carol has claimed that Jet was having affairs while she was pregnant. One of these, with a dancer, allegedly took place while she was hospitalised after the accident. After the birth of their baby, Ricky Brian, in the spring of 1960, he allegedly had a fling with a woman called Pauline from Sheffield. By this time, their marriage was effectively over.

On tour

After a short break, Cliff and the Shadows flew to the USA in January 1960 for a gruelling 38-day whistle-stop tour with Irvin Feld's *Biggest Show of Stars for 1960 – Winter Edition* package. It was a fabulous bill featuring Johnny & The Hurricanes, Freddy Cannon, Bobby Rydell, Clyde McPhatter – a founder member of the US Drifters (I wonder if anyone discussed the copyright on the Drifters name with him!), Sammy Turner, the Clovers, the Isley Brothers, and Frankie Avalon headlining (he'd racked up two Top Ten Hits in 1958 with 'Dede Dinah' and 'Gingerbread' and two Number Ones in 1959 with 'Venus' and 'Why').

Cliff (& The Shadows), who had been booked on the strength of US chart success with 'Living Doll', were advertised as *'England's #1 Singing Sensation'* and also as *'Cliff Richard and The Shadows – An Added Attraction from Britain'*. At most shows Cliff opened the second half with a 15-minute spot singing 'Whole Lotta Shakin' Goin' On', 'My Babe', 'Forty Days', 'Living Doll' and his current UK release, 'Voice In The Wilderness', from the movie *Expresso Bongo*. He went down well in the main, but there was a view that the US didn't need to import British singers copying American rock'n'roll. Of course, there was no solo spot for his backing band.

The tour, which started in Montreal, Canada, criss-crossed the States for thousands of miles. The distances on UK tours must have seemed like short London taxi stops by comparison. Cities, towns and sights they had only read about a few years back were now a reality – to say nothing of the culture shock. It must have been a particularly wearying trip for Cliff's father, Rodger, who accompanied them, but the American market was a prize worth pursuing. Inexplicably, EMI seem to have done little else to push his US career. Perhaps they simply decided that the odds

The Shadows
Clockwise from left: Jet, Bruce, Tony and Hank.

were stacked against them.

During the tour, Cliff briefly returned to the UK to appear on TV's *Sunday Night at the London Palladium* to publicise 'Voice In The Wilderness'. If the Shadows needed any reminder that they were simply hired hands as far as Tito Burns was concerned, then this was it. On the Palladium show, Cliff was backed by the Parker Royal Four.

Back in the UK, Jet returned to Stockton-on-Tees for his court case. It was reported in the papers that he was fined £35.15.0 for dangerous driving, failure to display 'L' plates and having no qualified driver in the vehicle (at that time, he had not yet passed his driving test). Hank Marvin and tour manager Mike Conlin were also fined smaller amounts for aiding and abetting him.

In April, Cliff & The Shadows hit the road again for a tour of the UK. It was during this tour that singer-songwriter Jerry Lordan, who was also on the show thanks to his recent hits, 'I'll Stay Single' and 'Who Could Be Bluer', played them his new composition, 'Apache', on his ukelele. He told them he'd already offered the tune to guitarist Bert Weedon, but nothing had happened (Weedon had in fact recorded his version in January, but his record company, Top Rank, hadn't released it). This was an incredible stroke of luck for the Shadows, and one which would launch them on the path to stardom in their own right.

On 16 May, Cliff & The Shadows played a *Royal Variety Performance* at London's Victoria Palace Theatre, and on Friday, 3 June they opened a six-month season at the London Palladium.

The Palladium show was called *Stars In Your Eyes* and also featured Russ Conway, the popular pianist who had recently topped the charts with 'Side Saddle', 'Roulette' and 'China Tea', Billy Dainty, a favourite comedian of the Queen Mother, actor David Kossoff, at that time enjoying great popularity as 'Pa Larkin' in *The Larkins* TV comedy series, Canadian singer Edmund Hockridge, UK songstress Joan Regan and a young compère/comedian called Des O'Connor.

Given the short shelf life forecast for rock'n'roll, recasting Cliff as a popular entertainer in the eyes of the public must have looked like a smart move from promoter Bernard Delfont's point of view, and that of Cliff's manager, Tito Burns. Tommy Steele had already jumped the Good Ship Rock some time ago, and Presley, who had courted Las Vegas as far back as 1956, was now hot property in Hollywood.

The Shadows had no spot of their own and, in fairness, no claim to one when the show opened. Their job for six months, apart from any independent Sunday concerts at other venues, was simply to back Cliff. By any standards this was a very long season and must have been particularly boring for the boys, who, like Cliff, were previously used to the odd week at a theatre here or there sandwiched between strings of one-nighters. The artists were contracted to thirteen shows a week: twice-nightly at 6.15 and 8.45 with an additional matinée performance each Saturday at 2.40. Sunday morning must have been bliss, and a long time in coming around each week.

This sedate and cosy 'family show' promoted by Leslie A. MacDonnell and Bernard Delfont must have been something of an ordeal for the group, who were now more used to playing to hordes of screaming fans. In the main, weeknight audiences were lukewarm to the new music on this traditional variety bill, and the reception for Cliff and the boys would only liven up at the weekends, when the proportion of teenagers in the audience was greater.

The Marlborough Head pub opposite the Palladium was a favourite haunt of artists waiting to go on, or relaxing after their spot. Here, largely unbothered by fans and autograph collectors, they could unwind with a drink and a game of billiards. Tony Meehan was still under drinking age, and Bruce and Hank were apparently happy with cups of tea, but it provided a haven for Jet who, like the theatre's regular bandsmen, had bar breaks and re-entry to the theatre timed to the second.

Breakthrough!

On 17 June, a couple of weeks into their Palladium residency, the Shadows went into the studio to cut 'Apache', which had now been given a dramatic arrangement. Cliff came along too, and ended up playing the drum intro on 'Apache' and guitar on the flip, 'Quartermaster's Stores'. It would appear that the Shadows' version of 'Apache' and Bert Weedon's were released a week apart in mid-July, but there is some dispute as to which appeared first.

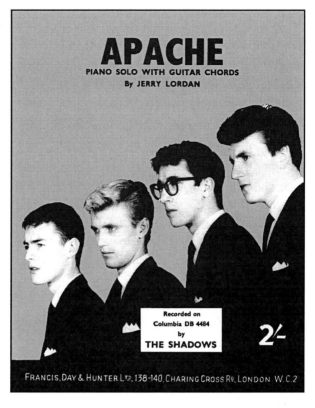

On 20 July, the Shadows' single entered the charts at No.19. Three weeks later it was at No.1, having deposed Cliff's 'Please Don't Tease'. Within the short space of two months or so, the Shadows had gone from being a backing band to a star act with the top single in the UK! (Weedon's release fared reasonably well too, charting one week after the Shadows and climbing to a respectable No.24 in August.)

There had been no basis for giving the Shadows a separate spot when the show was devised and timed, as they were merely Cliff's backing band; now they were the top act in the country. Amazingly, that's how things remained for the rest of the long season. With staggering inflexibility and short-sightedness, the promoters and management refused to make any changes to the programme, even though the show still had months to run. Fans who wanted to hear the new idols of British pop play their hit had to attend hastily-arranged Sunday night concerts or be content with the recording.

Despite their success in Britain, there was to be no US hit for the Shadows with 'Apache', as EMI failed to secure sufficient promotion for it when it was released over there on the Capitol label. Fortunately for composer Jerry Lordan, Danish guitarist

Jørgen Ingmann picked it up from a demo and recorded his own interpretation. Originally released as a 'B' side, it became a major hit for him, peaking at No.2 in the *Billboard* 'Hot 100' in April 1961. Had the Shadows' version cracked the US charts instead of Ingmann's, who knows where their career might have taken them over the next few years.

After 'Apache' it was still 'Cliff Richard & The Shadows', but the four lads now had their own identity, fan following, and importantly for their future earnings – solid worth to promoters. However, as members of Cliff's backing group, they were still on a weekly wage of just £25 each!

The time had come for them to look for a manager of their own who would look after their interests and guide their careers. Norrie Paramor pointed them towards Peter Gormley, an Australian who had recently moved to London to guide singer Frank Ifield's career. Gormley quickly gained a good reputation in the business and the Shadows thankfully landed in a safe pair of hands.

Even with their new and ever-growing popularity, there were some people the Shadows couldn't please. Cliff's, and to a lesser extent the Shadows' appeal to the girls enraged boyfriends. They would even come down to the front of the stage when they were playing and make 'V' signs.

When Cliff & The Shadows played Chiswick Empire Theatre for one week in late April 1959, two rival gangs of Teddy boys decided to fight it out in the gallery on Friday night during the second house. The support acts bravely attempted to do their spots, but very quickly missiles from upstairs began landing in the stalls and on the stage.

Comedian/compère Des O'Connor tried to calm things down, but they weren't having any of it. Ventriloquist Ray Alan was also on the bill, and it was his quick thinking in dropping the safety curtain down on the show that saved the cast and their equipment from injury and damage. That riot had nothing to do with Cliff & The Shadows, but such was Cliff's popularity with the girls that they often had pennies, eggs, tomatoes and vegetables thrown by jealous boyfriends.

Many older professional musicians were also jealous and condescending to these young upstarts. Others, like Bert Weedon, Don Lang and Harry Robinson (in the guise of Lord Rockingham's XI), simply decided to follow the trend.

It was also during the Palladium residency that matters between Carol, Jet and Cliff finally came to a head. After the latest of many rows, Carol took baby Ricky and walked out on Jet. In *Cliff Richard, The Bachelor Boy*, Carol claims that, on the night in question, Jet had hit her in the mouth and drawn blood, which Cliff saw afterwards when he drove her and baby Ricky to her mother's house.

Not long after, Cliff's mother accidentally intercepted a very personal letter from Carol and her son's relationship was swiftly brought to an end. Dorothy and Rodger Webb were not the type of parents to condone their son conducting an affair with a married woman, and had the story made it into the newspapers, Cliff's carefully-built career and promising future would have suffered irreparable damage. For a start, Bernard Delfont and the Grades would have dropped him like a hot brick. Apart from a clean image and scandal-proof life, pop idols had to be 'attainable' to the legions of female fans who thronged their concerts, put their records in the charts and bought their merchandise. Business is business, and nowhere is that more true than in show business. Unable to face Carol, Cliff asked Tony Meehan to break the news to her.

Tony once said that Cliff was a determined person who never put friendship before business, and clearly this extended to intimate friendship. It also shows Cliff's inability – readily admitted by him over the years – to confront people directly, no matter how close they may be to him. Meehan (who later studied psychology and psychiatry) was also of the opinion that Cliff's mother was so dominant in his life that this created a barrier to him having a normal relationship with any woman.

Although Tony was quite close to Jet and made no secret in later years of his dislike for Carol, it didn't prevent him assisting Cliff with the sleeper episode, or delivering Cliff's message that their relationship was finished. It should also be borne in mind that all the participants in this matter were just kids with little experience of life: they were all under the age of 20 at the time. During the period of the affair, Tony Meehan was a boy of 16 and 17.

'Apache' was such a massive hit that it was November before Columbia issued a follow-up. Although it did not hit the top, 'Man Of Mystery' *b/w* 'The Stranger' became a double-sided Top 5 smash. The Shadows were no 'one hit wonders'.

Not surprisingly, there were no pantomime appearances at the end of 1960. Cliff went off on holiday with his mum, while the Shadows sat on their laurels and rested up elsewhere.

Cliff gets married!

January 1961 saw the issue of the Shadows' first EP, which featured 'Mustang', 'Theme From Shane', 'Shotgun' and 'Theme From Giant'. It shot into the EP chart, where it stayed for a very respectable 47 weeks – 20 of them at No.1.

The policy of dramatic titles continued with the release of their third single, 'F.B.I.', in February, which reached No.6.

In March, Cliff and the Shadows visited South Africa, playing Bulawayo, Salisbury, Johannesburg, Port Elizabeth, Durban and Cape Town. According to contemporary press reports, some 3,000 fans turned out to welcome them at Johannesburg airport. Many more lined the route to their hotel, where a crowd of around 10,000 greeted them with cries of

Jet in South Africa.

'We want Cliff!'.

During the trip, Cliff and the boys were taken to visit a Zulu chief who, it turned out, was a huge fan of theirs (Cliff was very popular with blacks as well as whites). The chief treated them like royalty and put on a celebratory ceremony in which Cliff 'married' one of his many wives. No doubt to his great relief, he was not prevailed upon to consummate the union!

How these young lads, who numbered black American artists amongst their musical heroes and influences, viewed the segregation and inequalities prevailing in South Africa at that time can only be guessed at. However, it was reported that, when they discovered that they would be playing to an all-white audience because interracial mixing was not permitted under apartheid, they offered to do a second concert for black citizens and donate the proceeds to the Salisbury Society for Handicapped Africans.

After their return from Africa, Cliff and the Shadows rested up briefly before embarking upon another whistle-stop tour of UK theatres and cinemas in April for Arthur Howes.

The show was opened by a mature trio calling themselves the Wiseguys. They were followed by Norman Vaughan, a time-served comedian who had appeared with Harry Secombe in *Rockin' The Town* at the Palladium and was another artist being groomed for the top; a female trio called the Sonnettes, and singer Patti Brook (winner of the 1960 *Soho Fair Disc Competition*). The Shadows rounded off the first half, as befitted their new status.

Backstage in Halifax, 1961.

After the interval it was the Wiseguys again, followed by 'Britain's answer to the Everlys', the Brook Brothers, whose catchy 'Warpaint' was heading up the charts at the time. Cliff closed the show, backed of course by the Shadows, after which the audience was expected to stand respectfully while 'God Save The Queen' was played over the PA system. The acts were changing, but the old variety tradition was still alive and well.

By the time the tour ended, Jet and Patti Brook were an item (and would remain so for the best part of three years), and the Shadows' new single, 'Frightened City', was in the charts. It peaked at No.3 in June. Their second EP, *Shadows To The Fore*, featuring the winning combination of 'Apache', 'Man Of Mystery', 'The Stranger' and 'F.B.I.', entered the EP chart that same month to stay for an amazing 81 weeks – 28 of them at No.1.

Cliff was doing well too – 'Please Don't Tease', 'Nine Times Out Of Ten', 'I Love You', 'Theme For A Dream' and 'Gee Whiz It's You' all made the Top 5 between June 1960 and May 1961 – but his good fortune was soured by the untimely death of his father, Rodger, on 15 May. However, he had little time to grieve, as his career was now proceeding at a relentless pace. Shooting for *The Young Ones*, his third movie, commenced almost immediately, but he also had to squeeze in appearances on *Thank Your Lucky Stars* and the *Billy Cotton Band Show* to promote his latest single, 'A Girl Like You', which made No.3 in July.

In June, while their boss spent the weekend filming *The Young Ones,* the Shadows joined other bands and some two thousand fans to take part in *Rock Across The Channel* – a return Sunday trip from Gravesend to Calais on the MV *Royal Daffodil.* Cliff's three sisters joined the boat at Southend. The floating rock'n'roll concert received much publicity, but members of the press intent on the sensational reporting of bad teenage behaviour went back to their newspapers disappointed.

In August, Cliff undertook a short tour of Scandinavia with the Shadows shortly before the start of their summer season at Blackpool Opera House.

September saw EMI release the Shadows' first LP, *The Shadows*, which saw their Goons-style humour reflected in titles like 'See You In My Drums' and 'Theme From A Filleted Place'. Available in both mono and stereo, it stormed into the LP chart for a 57-week run and made No.1. That same month, their new single, 'Kon-Tiki' entered the charts and also hit the top spot.

Jet also passed his driving test, and treated himself to a new Volvo.

Cracks in the wall

On the surface, everything looked fine, but relationships within the group were becoming increasingly strained. The constant touring, too few days off, the domestic pressures of newly-weds and babies, and the irritations associated with living in each others' pockets for much of the year were all beginning to take their toll. Hank was pretty easy-going by nature, but Bruce was both a worrier and a perfectionist. The boys had come a long way in a very short time and he was determined that they should stay successful – and who can blame him?

Tony Meehan's propensity for showing up late for performances worried him greatly. During the Blackpool season, and after frequent rows, the 18-year-old quit the group (the usual 'musical differences' reason was cited) and went to work as an A&R man for Decca. He was quickly replaced by Brian Bennett, former house drummer at the 2I's and member of Marty Wilde's Wildcats.

Jet was likewise beginning to cause Bruce serious concern. Although he could be great fun (for example, when the fans screamed for Cliff outside a theatre, Jet would jokingly shout out of a dressing room window: 'Cliff's queer and he hates his fans!'), his drinking and erratic behaviour were rapidly becoming a liability. On one occasion, the Shadows were performing at Liverpool's famous Cavern Club doing their synchronised 'walk' when Jet fell into the audience. Bruce attempted to explain that their bass player wasn't well, but people in the audience shouted back: 'He's pissed!'

In Steve Turner's *Cliff Richard, The Bachelor Boy*, Ron King (variously Cliff's bus driver, tour manager and personal assistant) recalled that Jet and Bruce were always quarrelling because Bruce couldn't stand Jet's drinking, and that Sam Curtis, their roadie, had had to look after Jet more than the others because he needed it.

In the same book, Hank Marvin stated that Jet, who saw himself as a James Dean character, could be mean and moody, as well as a lot of fun. 'Moody' seems to come up a lot when people have described Jet.

Given the direction his life would later take, Royston Ellis's portrait of Jet in 1961's *The Big Beat Scene* was also prophetically accurate:

'Undoubtedly Jet Harris is the Shadow with the most sex appeal. His hungry look, dark, sunken eyes and fiery performance help him to coax screams from an audience with just a smile. Offstage he is little different from the image his fans love. He is an exhibitionist and must always have an audience to draw him out.

'In that slim body of his burns a fantastic energy, which leaves an impression on all who meet him. Coming from an

The new Shadows line-up.
Left to right: Brian Bennett, Bruce, Jet and Hank.

ordinary home background himself, he loves the unusual, the offbeat, the kinky people who, he reckons, are the most interesting in the world. Studying them, he likes to discover what made them tick, adopting their interesting characteristics for himself.

'One of his favourite London characters is the poetess Iris Orton, known around Soho for her experiments with poetry and music. Jet himself has been involved with similar experiments with poetry and music. In 1959, he composed the pop music backing to poems that were performed by the Shadows on television with the author of this book.

'In pursuit of enjoyment and knowledge, Jet leads a pretty hectic life. His 21st birthday in 1960 was celebrated in a riotous fashion. With a friend to drive his car, armed with a bottle of strong wine, Jet set off for a prowl around London's coffee bars after his evening's stint at the Palladium. Picking up friends *en route*, the evening developed into a party on wheels. Jet flaked out in his flat about five the next morning.

'Jet is a rare personality to find in show business. Not only is he a talented musician, he is a genuine person with a sense of justice and a strong loyalty to his friends. He is able to ferret out the best in everyone and encourage it. Occasionally, he has a wildness about him bordering on immaturity. His bouts of erratic behaviour make his position as a star name very difficult. Unable to appreciate responsibilities, he likes a steady person at his side to keep an eye on him.

'On the scene they say that Jet Harris will not live beyond 30. Whenever he dies, Jet will have experienced more in life than the average person. And he will long be remembered as a legend in the sometimes sordid world of musicians, poets and offbeats he likes so much.'

I quit!

On 15 October 1961, the day after his 21st birthday, Cliff and the new Shadows line-up set off on a tour of Singapore, Australia (where they played Sydney, Melbourne, Perth and Adelaide) and New Zealand. Meanwhile the hits continued to flow.

Cliff's 'When The Girl In Your Heart Is The Girl In Your Arms' made the Top 5 later that month, while the Shadows' latest, 'The Savage', made the Top 10 in November. Their performance of 'The Savage' was also one of the most memorable moments of *The Young Ones* film, released on 19 December to rave reviews. Within a week, the soundtrack album was in the charts heading for No.1.

At the end of 1961, the Shadows – without Cliff this time – paid a return visit to Stockton's Globe Theatre to play 'the Broker's Men' in the pantomime *Dick Whittington*, starring comedian Ken Platt as Idle Jack and Frank Ifield as Dick. The panto ran from Christmas Day – which fell on a Monday that year – for three weeks, and was well received.

1962 got off to a good start, with Cliff's 'Young Ones' single shooting to No.1 in January, and the Shadows' latest, 'Wonderful Land' repeating the performance in March. At this

point in their career, Cliff and the Shadows were truly on top of their game.

On 15 April, they appeared at the prestigious *NME Poll Winners Concert* at Wembley's Empire Pool, as they'd won in three categories: Cliff had been selected best 'British Male Singer' with 18,006 votes; the Shadows had topped the 'British Small Group' poll with a massive 45,951 votes; and Jet had won 'Solo Instrumentalist' with 20,955 votes (interestingly, Hank Marvin, who to many was *the* solo instrumentalist, didn't even make the top three: Acker Bilk claimed second spot with 13,911 votes and Bert Weedon romped in to third position with 9,087!). The Shadows were also presented, somewhat belatedly, with a gold disc for sales of 'Apache'. Jet did the show and then walked out.

Bruce Welch says he was sacked, while Jet claimed that he resigned. The exact truth may never be known, but it would certainly have been legally difficult for one or two founder members to sack a third. What is evident, is that Jet was drinking heavily and in an emotional state – so whether his sudden departure was planned or spontaneous is debatable. Most likely it is something he had been thinking about for a while, then did on the spur of the moment. But, if showbiz management were encouraging him to jump ship, then they were not acting responsibly to a young man whose emotional and alcohol problems, which would have been well known to them by that time, were already too much for him to cope with.

Having announced former Vince Eager and Marty Wilde sideman Brian 'Licorice' Locking as Jet's replacement, Shadows manager Peter Gormley – who was by now also managing Cliff – was quoted in *Disc* as saying, 'It is something he has wanted to do for a long time. It has always been a question of when. The moment came just before Easter when the Shadows had a break from engagements. The last thing that the boys and myself would wish to do is stand in the way of Jet realising his ambition. He has the good wishes of Hank, Bruce, Brian, Cliff and myself.'

Almost immediately, several newspapers cited television producer, showbiz Svengali and Decca A&R man Jack Good as Jet's new manager. Two weeks later, Jet signed with Decca. (The fact that he could so easily switch from EMI to Decca indicates that it was the Shadows as a group entity who were signed to EMI, rather than the individual members.) It subsequently transpired that Jet had appointed Jack Good as his *recording* manager and musical director, and Roy Moseley of the Delfont Organisation as his personal manager.

Good certainly had the magic touch, and under his guidance Jet recorded 'Besame Mucho' and 'Chills And Fever' at the label's Portland Place studio, playing lead on a six-string bass guitar. Arranged by Charles Blackwell and produced by Good, 'Besame' was an immediate hit in May 1962, but only reached a disappointing No.22.

Speaking to Brian Gibson of *Disc*, Jet was nevertheless upbeat: 'I think that we could have picked a better number, but for the fact that we were pressed for time... but on the whole I think my first record did well and I'm pleased with the reaction to it.' He added: 'I'm perfectly happy with my decision to leave the Shadows, and as far as my future

---

THE FANTASTIC NEW SOUND OF

JET HARRIS

BESAME MUCHO   CHILLS & FEVER

published by
SOUTHERN MUSIC
8 Denmark St.
London W C2

recorded on
45 rpm **DECCA** F 11466

published by
BELINDA (LONDON) LTD
17 Savile Row
London W 1

---

is concerned I'm confident that things will work out well.'

In the same interview, Jet also enthused about his new instrument: 'The public haven't heard half the sounds that this instrument can produce, and I think the bass guitar is going to mean a lot to them. It's a mean sound that the boys will go for more than the girls.'

The 1963 *NME Annual* carried a full-page feature titled JET HARRIS BEATS THE CRITICS outlining in a rather inaccurate chronology his transition from leader of the Shadows and national personality to successful solo artist. Bert Weedon, one of his rivals in the *NME* poll, was quoted as saying, 'I think he is wise to go solo: this way he is set to become a star in his own right.'

This article and others in the music press also reported that Jet was keen to get into acting, and that TV and film opportunities were waiting for him. One paper stated that his first movie role would be the lead in *Tom Sawyer*, to be made by 'an independent company'.

The launch of pop's new golden boy continued with information that Jet had been offered a dramatic role in an episode of Associated Rediffusion's popular TV crime series, *No Hiding Place* (starring Raymond Francis and Eric Lander) and that, if he accepted the role, it would be a major break for him in his new career.

In a 'question-and-answer' feature in *NME*, Jet revealed: 'We have two really hot film roles on offer at the moment, but the trouble is that we can't make up our minds between them. But things are definitely moving and I feel quite optimistic. And

49

The 'mean, moody and magnificent' Jet Harris, 1962.

taking lessons from Albert Finney's drama teacher is helping me tremendously. As for ambitions – well, I'm not the type who could play in a film like *The Young Ones*. I'd like to go for the moody roles – that would give me a chance to be myself, because people are always telling me that I'm moody. But I don't mean anything as drastic as the James Dean-Marlon Brando type of parts. They're too way out for my liking!'

As to whether he would cease to be a guitarist if he became a successful actor or singer, he replied: 'Not on your life! This is really my first love, and I'm sure it will always be. Today, when I have any spare time, I go along and sit in at jazz clubs – just for kicks'.

It was also reported that, following a three-day engagement in Amsterdam, Jet had been offered a return booking at a major venue there. This was to follow a show he was due to headline at the Olympia Theatre in Paris, probably at the end of November. Even allowing for the planted hype so beloved of the popular music industry, things were looking rosy for Jet – workwise at least.

Out of the frying pan

However, there was still much work to be done. Recording in a studio with regular musicians was one thing, but getting up on stage in front of an audience and being able to put on a good show was another matter entirely. A backing group, the Jetblacks, was formed, consisting of Barry Lovegrove on guitar, Dave 'Quincey' Quickendon on tenor sax, Glenn Hughes on baritone sax, Mick Underwood on drums and Patti Brook's brother, Terry Webster, on second bass guitar and harmony vocals. They spent the next few months rehearsing under Jack Good's direction in a studio near London's Piccadilly Circus that was formerly the Hippodrome Theatre.

Jet Harris & The Jetblacks made their television debut on Granada TV's *Spot The Tune* on 10 August 1962. On 19 August, they played their first live show at the Princess Theatre, Torquay. The popular vocal trio, the Mudlarks, who'd enjoyed a UK hit with a cover of the Chordettes' record, 'Lollipop', were the main support. The *NME* announced that 'plans for Jet's round-the-world-tour, first revealed in the *NME* on June 15, are nearing completion; he will embark on a tour of at least a dozen countries early next year.'

August also saw the release of the follow-up to 'Besame Mucho', and again Jet and Jack Good were shown to have exercised sound judgement. Their main selection was another instrumental, 'Main Title Theme (from 'Man With The Golden Arm')' *b/w* 'Some People', a vocal side. The movie, *The Man With The Golden Arm,* starring Frank Sinatra, had been a box office smash when shown in the UK during 1956, and Elmer Bernstein's memorable theme, recorded by big bands and reinforced via radio play requests, was well impressed upon the public consciousness, so Decca were off to a good head start. The record made No.12 in September.

Having demonstrated to management – and, more importantly, to concert promoters – that he could take the stage successfully as a solo act, Jet was booked for a short tour at the

Gene and Jet, 1963.

beginning of October with Del Shannon and Freddy Cannon, immediately followed by a 21-day nationwide tour promoted by Don Arden. Originally, Arden's show was to feature three American headliners: Little Richard, Sam Cooke and Gene Vincent. Unfortunately for Gene's fans, his work permit had run out and officially he was banned from performing on any UK stage until the spring of 1963. Thankfully, this problem for Arden surfaced early on, and when the concert posters and flyers went out the joint headliners were shown as Little Richard, Sam Cooke and Jet Harris (& The Jetblacks).

The tour opened at Doncaster on 8 October, but Sam Cooke missed the show due to his plane being delayed. However, the wily promoter had Gene on hand singing from the auditorium, and he continued to make this type of appearance throughout the tour. Much has been written about Don Arden after his death, but he could certainly put a show together and for many fans was *the*

British promoter when it came to presenting hit-making acts from the USA. At this time, Arden would have been taking a considerable risk in replacing the idol of the rockers, Gene Vincent, with an artist like Jet Harris and it's quite possible that he used Vincent's unscheduled 'surprise' appearances as his ace in the hole.

Jet was still drinking heavily. Plagued by pre-stage nerves throughout his career, he had probably failed to realise that standing out front as the star of the show would be considerably more stressful and uncomfortable than standing behind one as part of a group. It is a change he found difficult to adjust to, and it probably increased his reliance upon alcohol. On that tour he did however, find kindred spirits in Sam Cooke and, when he did appear, Gene Vincent.

After the tour had ended, Jet and his management decided to team him up on disc with his old pal from the Shadows, Tony Meehan. Perhaps Jet thought it would be less pressure to be one half of a duo, rather than a solo act. Although they hadn't kept in close touch, Tony, who now worked for Decca Records as an A&R man and producer, had played on Jet's solo records. Although he had some reservations ('Drink was Jet's downfall,' he later explained), Tony agreed.

Predictably, the reunion attracted a blaze of publicity and the boys were lucky enough to be offered the excellent Jerry Lordan composition, 'Diamonds'. Arranged and produced by Meehan, the instrumental owed more than a little to the Shadows' sound.

Needless to say, it was a massive hit, topping the hit parade for most of February 1963. Future Led Zeppelin guitarist Jimmy Page was booked to play

The dynamic duo on tour, 1963.

rhythm guitar on the session, which over the years has led to some speculation about what his actual contribution may have been. However, in *Cliff Richard, The Bachelor Boy*, Tony Meehan confirmed that Jet did play on 'Diamonds', though it took him two days to lay down the track.

On 9 February, Jet and Tony made their TV debut on the BBC's *Billy Cotton Band Show* and were presented with a silver disc for 250,000 sales of their record. They also appeared in the

No.1 No.1 No.1 No.1

DIAMONDS

JET HARRIS ☆ TONY MEEHAN

Thanks to everyone concerned for helping to make our first record together so successful.

pop music film, *Just For Fun*, released that month, with a lightweight vocal offering called '(Doing The) Hully Gully'. Jet also performed a solo number, 'Man From Nowhere', with the Jetblacks. Shot in darkness, with dramatic uplighting, it was one of the most memorable moments of the picture.

There were also big changes afoot in Jet's personal life at this time. While at ABC TV's studios on 17 February to film an appearance for the following Saturday's *Thank Your Lucky Stars*, he met pretty 17-year-old singer Billie Davis. Billie had partnered Mike Sarne on his 1962 hit, 'Will I What', and now had a chart record in her own right with 'Tell Him'. Jet was smitten. Unfortunately, things were somewhat complicated by the fact that he already had a steady girlfriend, Patti Brook, and was still married to Carol (although she was by now taking action to divorce him).

A few days later, on 20 February, the *Daily Express* informed its readers that Jet was in a Harley Street nursing home and quoted his manager, Roy Moseley, as saying, 'He is suffering from nervous exhaustion and has been told to take a complete rest'.

In March, Jet & Tony went out on the road as part of an Arthur Howes tour featuring Gene Vincent, John Leyton, the Voltairs, Johnny Temple and Patti Brook. After wrestling with his conscience for some time, Jet decided to end his two-year relationship with Patti, who, needless to say, was devastated. Shortly after, he set up home with Billie at 77 Portsea Hall in Marble Arch, London.

For their follow-up to 'Diamonds', Jerry Lordan came up with another winner in the shape of 'Scarlett O'Hara', which stopped just short of the top slot at No.2 in the last week of May. In May and June, the boys went out on tour again, this time with John Leyton, the Four Seasons, Mike Berry, Billie Davis and Duffy Power.

'I have to admit that things have not gone exactly as I had planned,' Jet confessed to the *NME*'s Derek Johnson. 'When Tony and I recorded 'Diamonds', we looked upon it as a one-shot novelty, and we didn't dream that it would be such a success.

Now, we're determined to carry on together. We've got to – the fans expect it.'

In the same interview, Jet was also at pains to point out that he was no longer a bass guitarist: 'That's a thing of the past. Most people don't seem to realise that I've switched to ordinary guitar now. And that's the way it's going to stay – I doubt if I shall ever go back to the bass guitar. You remember when I first launched out on my own, I was playing a six-string bass guitar on 'Besame Mucho'? That was all very well, but I found that it restricted my playing enormously. So now I've switched to pukka guitar – but it's tuned down one tone in order to give it a deeper sound.'

On the last day of August, Jet & Tony made a high-profile appearance on a *Thank Your Lucky Stars 'Summer Spin'* TV special, to plug their new single, 'Applejack'. The record hit No.4 in September. Three great singles, three smashes.

It was only years later that the truth came out. Guitarist Joe Moretti takes up the story:

'In 1963, I quit Nero & The Gladiators after recording 'Bleak House' – the follow-up to 'Hall Of The Mountain King' – and joined the Jet Harris/Tony Meehan band. The original line-up for that band was: Tony Meehan, drums; Jet, six-string bass guitar; John Paul Jones (John Baldwin), bass guitar; Glenn Hughes, baritone sax; Chris Hughes, tenor sax, flute, arranger; and myself on guitar.

'Just to keep the "records" straight, Jet didn't feature on 'Scarlett O'Hara' and 'Applejack' – I did. Jet was too "ill" at the time. He just couldn't function any more, and was going through a lot of personal problems including a divorce.

'Why did I do it? Well, I really felt sorry for Jet. He was a helluva nice guy, and the danger was that, if I hadn't cut those tracks, the whole band could have fallen apart and six guys would have been out of work. I got an extra £5 a week to keep my mouth shut, and I needed the money to support my wife and child. The hurtful thing about that period is that, in his articles, Meehan doesn't even mention that I was a member of the band. As if I had never existed! So, I got a wage while Meehan laughed all the way to the bank.'

Indeed, during this golden period of professional success Jet & Tony were estimated to be earning £1,000 per week each – a far cry from their early days as wage-earning players with the Shadows. But then, having Jet & Tony on the bill was good insurance for any promoter.

On the strength of their latest hit, they were booked for a 28-date Arthur Howes tour in October featuring Del Shannon, Gerry & The Pacemakers, the Bachelors, Duffy Power and Cilla Black.

The Crash

Disaster struck with a vengeance on 10 September 1963. Jet had been to the Savoy Hotel in London to receive a couple of *NME* awards (including 'Musician of the Year'), after which he and Billie travelled to Evesham, Worcestershire, where Billie was due to perform that evening.

On the way back home, their chauffeur-driven limousine collided with a Midland Red bus at a road junction. Jet was knocked unconscious and suffered severe head injuries requiring 34 stitches; Billie sustained torn leg muscles and splinter fractures on both sides of her jaw, which had to be wired for several months. (It was also widely reported that Jet had injured his left hand, as he was seen wearing a bandage. In actual fact, he'd hurt his hand a week earlier when he accidentally broke a window.) Despite her injuries, Billie managed to drag Jet out of the vehicle to safety.

In the *Daily Express* of 12 September Jet commented: 'It was a carbon copy of the one we had not long ago[*]. A chauffeur was driving and Billie and I were asleep in the back, just as we were doing last time.'

As if the accident wasn't bad enough, details of their affair were splashed all over the popular press. A number of commentators voiced their strong disapproval of young ladies consorting with married men, and Billie took the full force of

---

[*] In July 1963.

their vitriol. Jet did his best to defend her, explaining that he was separated and awaiting a divorce but, in addition to their physical and mental injuries, their reputations and careers had already been damaged.

On 14 September, Jet's manager, Roy Moseley was quoted by the *Daily Express* as stating – somewhat over-optimistically – that Jet hoped to be playing again in about ten days' time. Indeed, it would appear that, with 'Applejack' high in the charts, there was a lot of

Billie Davis.

pressure put on Jet to resume playing before he had properly recovered. Just three weeks after the horrific crash that almost claimed his life, he was booked to appear on *Ready Steady Go!* – with predictable consequences.

JET HARRIS IN 'I'LL QUIT SHOWBIZ' SENSATION announced the *Daily Mirror* of 5 October 1963: 'Top guitarist Jet Harris created a sensation last night. He walked out of a TV show saying: "I've finished with show business." It happened just after he arrived at Associated Rediffusion's London studios to appear in *Ready Steady Go!* His partner, drummer Tony Meehan, went on without him...

'Last night Jet and Tony should have appeared at the Odeon, Lewisham. But Jet Harris did not turn up. A spokesman for the Bernard Delfont organisation, which handles their business affairs, said last night: "The whole thing is a mess. We don't know what's happening. We can't find Jet Harris since he walked out of the TV studio.'"

On 7 October, the *Daily Express* reported that Jet had been discovered in a Brighton flat: 'He was in bed, under sedation – too ill to see anybody.' The friend he was staying with, Steve Lindsey, was quoted as saying that Jet was 'completely shattered by a nervous breakdown. Show business and the recent car crash have made him a wreck.'

The *Daily Mirror* ran a similar story on the same day titled JET HARRIS QUITS – 'NERVE HAS SNAPPED': 'All he would say about his future was: "Tell them I'm out for good. I've quit show business and am not coming back." Billie whispered: "He's on the verge of a nervous breakdown. He can't take it any longer. He's made up his mind to get out. He's been pushed too hard. His nerves have snapped. His hands are trembling and he takes sleeping pills. One thing is certain. He won't ever play again."'

Despite Jet's fragile condition – or perhaps because of it – the press were unrelenting in their coverage. On the morning of 8 October, the *Daily Mirror* ran a story about THE COUPLE WHO CAUGHT THE 10.25: 'Jet was taking the train to London and Harley Street yesterday to see his doctor... He sat in the train, his trembling fingers tugging the strands of a crumpled cigarette. He drank a brandy and port "to steady his nerves".

'"It wasn't the car crash that caused this breakdown," whispered Jet. "It only brought it on quicker. It was coming for a long time." He touched fresh scars on his nose and forehead and explained: "I got those when I collapsed in a lift yesterday. It was just a blackout."

'Last night, Jet, his medical check over, was told he must rest for six months. Still looking pale and exhausted, he caught his train back to Brighton.'

The same day's issue of the *Daily Express* reported that 'ashen-faced and trembling, the pop guitarist, Jet Harris, went to see his doctor yesterday. "I feel ill," he said. "I can't stop trembling and I don't know what it is."' The paper also mentioned that he went to see his parents in Willesden, who must by now have been beside themselves with worry.

On 10 October, Jet was arrested on Brighton seafront for being drunk and disorderly. The *Daily Mirror* of 12 October reported the outcome of the previous day's court hearing: 'Jet Harris, £1,000-a-week pop guitarist may never again be able to perform in public, a court was told yesterday... His solicitor, Mr David Jacobs, told the court that five weeks ago Harris was involved in a crash as a car passenger. He received serious brain and head injuries and had been unable to work since. Mr Jacobs added that Harris was suffering from neurosis and depression after the accident. He had been prescribed sedatives and "very unwisely" drank some beer after taking some of his tablets. Harris pleaded guilty and was fined £4.'

Covering the same story, the *Daily Express* added: 'His doctor confirmed that he was on the verge of a nervous breakdown... Mr Jacobs said: "He is going to spend the rest of the day in bed. He's a very sick boy. He's got to rest."'

Tony Meehan, meanwhile, had no option but to soldier on – not least because of his contractual obligations to tour promoter Arthur Howes. The Jet Harris/Tony Meehan band was quickly restyled 'The Tony Meehan Combo', with Joe Moretti moving up to play lead and John McLaughlin being recruited to play rhythm. After missing the first week due to Tony Meehan's illness, they covered all the remaining Jet & Tony dates.

They even managed a minor hit with 'Song of Mexico' in January 1964, but the group disintegrated soon after, as Moretti explains: 'Oh, what a change came over that band. Within a month *[of John McLaughlin joining]* we had transformed our repertoire, apart from our two chart hits. Jazz took over from the pile of shite we were playing up until then. Of course, the kids came to hear our pop music, and when they didn't get it, they started to stay away. Within a couple of months there were no more bookings. The band folded soon after that.'

The lost years

Early in 1964, posters proclaimed *'The Return of Jet Harris'* on the *All Stars '64* package, which began touring the UK on 8 February. The series of one-nighters also featured John Leyton, the Rolling Stones, Mike Sarne, Billie Davis and Mike Berry & The Innocents. The Innocents (formerly Bobby Angelo & The Tuxedos) also provided backup for Jet on tour and at the *NME Poll Winners Concert* in April, where he performed 'Diamonds' and his latest single, 'Big Bad Bass'. Written by the prolific Carter-Lewis team, it had been released by Decca in February to tie in with the tour, but failed to sell. Musical tastes had moved on, and the era of the big guitar sound was over.

Sadly, Jet's comeback attempt was short-lived and he quickly slipped back into a chaotic, alcohol-fuelled lifestyle that constantly kept his name in the papers over the next couple of years – usually for all the wrong reasons.

On 23 March 1964, the *Daily Mirror* reported that 'Jet Harris was taken to hospital yesterday after singer Billie Davis, 19, broke off their romance and planned marriage. Harris, 24, who made his comeback after a nervous breakdown less than two months ago, was rushed to St Mary's Hospital, Paddington, unconscious. He had "minor injuries". Last night, he returned to his flat in Portsea Place and would not see callers... Billie nursed Jet through a nervous breakdown eight months ago – and starred with him in a pop show which began early in February. They went on a nationwide tour, and returned only three weeks ago.'

The very next day, the *Daily Mirror* proclaimed: POP ROMANCE ON THE ROCKS: 'I'VE LEFT JET' – BILLIE: 'Pop singer Billie Davis, her eyes red from weeping, said last night: "It wasn't really love – I was just his nursemaid. I couldn't go on a minute longer."'

Clearly, the strain of looking after Jet had become too much. However, the split proved to be only temporary. The *Daily Sketch* of 4 May 1964 reported that BILLIE & JET ARE TOGETHER AGAIN.

On 8 June 1964, Jet became a free man once more. The *Daily Mirror* reported that 'Guitarist Jet Harris, 24, offered no

defence when his wife, Carol, 23, was given a decree nisi because of his cruelty and adultery. The judge exercised discretion in respect of Mrs Harris's adultery.'

Had the divorce been finalised before the crash, then things might have been very different for Jet and Billie. As it was, it made little difference.

On 9 March 1965, the *Daily Mirror* informed its readers that 'Jet Harris was charged at Paddington last night with common assault. He will appear in court today.'

Police had been called to deal with a disturbance and discovered Jet pointing a shotgun at five people, whom he had herded into a porter's lodge at the Portsea Hall flats where he lived with Billie. He had been drinking. Giving evidence, a CID officer stated: 'Some time ago, Harris had a car accident and he is now not quite sound in the mind. The shotgun was not loaded. It had been used in a pantomime.'

In his defence, Jet explained it had just been a 'joke', adding: 'Look, I'm a musician. I don't shoot people.'

The magistrate, Mr Geoffrey Raphael, responded: 'On the face of it, it looks like some mental trouble.' A probation officer confirmed that Jet was being treated by a psychiatrist and was due to see him again the following day.

He was fined £5.

Within hours Jet's romance with Billie was over. The 'shotgun' incident seems to have been the final straw. Considering her tender years – she was still only 19 at the time – Billie had coped admirably with some extremely challenging situations over the past eighteen months. She had been publicly castigated for being 'the other woman' and associating with a married man – never mind that he hadn't seen his wife for years and that she'd had nothing to do with breaking up the relationship. She had paid a heavy price, emotionally and in career terms, for loving, nursing and sticking by Jet Harris. However, despite all her efforts, his drinking was becoming more extreme, his behaviour more erratic and his lifestyle more chaotic. In the end, she had to escape for the sake of her own sanity.

Following his break-up with Billie, Jet moved out of Portsea Hall and in the months that followed lived at various addresses in the capital, attempting to hold down different jobs outside of show business – even if it was just to pay for alcohol.

On 25 May 1965, the *Daily Mirror* reported that 'Jet Harris, 26, was fined £16 and disqualified from driving for a year at Marylebone Court yesterday when he admitted driving while unfit through drink. The court was told that Harris, of Observatory Gardens, Kensington, hit two parked cars in his Land Rover.'

With his money running out, Jet decided to sell his story to the papers – something he was to do many times throughout his career. The first part of WHEN A POP IDOL FALLS – THE AGONY OF JET HARRIS appeared in *The People* on Sunday, 13 June. It was predictable stuff (*'Tough at the top? It was torture – and I'll tell you why!'*), but put some much-needed cash in his pocket.

That summer, in London, Jet met a barmaid from Cheltenham called Susan Speed, and within a couple of months they both moved out to her hometown to work in a pub there. They were married on 8 June 1966 at Cheltenham register office. The press recorded that Jet had taken a day off his £15-a-week job as a barman in order to attend.

Jet and Billie's crash compensation case was eventually heard by the High Court in late 1966. On 21 December, the papers reported that Jet had been awarded £11,150 and Billie £1,757. Jet's £11,150 consisted of £1,150 agreed medical expenses and £10,000 for 'pain and suffering, loss of status and loss of earning capacity'.

Mr Justice Donaldson acknowledged that, although he was 'no Beatle and possibly no Cliff Richard', Jet was 'nevertheless at the top of his profession'. He went on to elaborate that 'by "loss of status" I do not mean so much as a performer, but as an individual following the personality change from becoming an alcohol addict – though he took too much to drink anyway, from suffering from mental illness and consequently having to be confined.'

Many observers felt that the award did not adequately reflect the physical damage and mental suffering Jet had suffered, or his lost earnings (he'd been making an estimated £1,000 per week immediately before the crash). The judge rejected a suggestion from the defence that Jet was already burned out before the accident, drinking heavily and wanting to get out of show business, and that the accident was merely an excuse to do so. While giving evidence, Jet mentioned that he was trying to build up his confidence again by playing in small clubs using instruments given to him by the Shadows.

Just two days later, on 23 December 1966, Susan Harris filed for divorce. To her credit, she made no claim on the monies Jet had just been awarded for his injuries. The marriage was annulled in September 1967.

While eking out a living doing bar work and various labouring jobs, Jet still harboured dreams of getting back into the music business. Despite his well-known personal problems, he was tried out as bassist with the newly-formed Jeff Beck Group in February 1967, but his alcoholism was now too far gone and he was dropped after a few rehearsals. Interviewed by the BBC in 2001, he recalled what happened after he went out for a drink with Beck and Rod Stewart: 'I woke up in my car in the car park, and it was six o'clock. But the problem was, I didn't know if it was six o'clock in the morning – because it was winter, you know. I thought, *Now, is this morning or night?*'

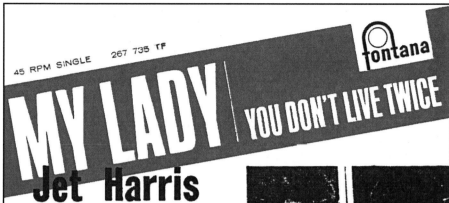

45 RPM SINGLE   267 735 TF

fontana

MY LADY | YOU DON'T LIVE TWICE

Jet Harris comeback

† "My Lady" (Fontana).

THIS is the Reg Presley song which was to have been a Troggs single, but was withdrawn at the last moment. Now it marks the comeback of ex-Shadows' bass guitarist, Jet Harris. And let me say right away that Jet's is much better than the Troggs' waxing.

It's loaded with surprises, not the least of which is the competent dual-tracked vocal. The arrangement is quite startling, with oscillating twangs, rasping brass, flutes and strange jungle noises. Good!

(New Musical Express)

After three-year absence JET HARRIS makes single comeback teamed again with fellow ex-Shadow TONY MEEHAN, now Jet's record producer and co-manager.

In the summer of that year, Larry Page, now a successful manager and producer, tried to revive Jet's career with a single on the Fontana label. A session with a 14-piece orchestra and Tony Meehan as producer was arranged for 15 June. The record came out a month later.

'My Lady' was a new sound for Jet, with a gentle, woodwindy opening and a second vocalist, Peter Gage, singing harmonies. The song had originally been written by Reg Presley for the Troggs, but had never been released. Maybe the Troggs knew something Jet didn't, as it vanished without trace. Although he still had a loyal fan following, the pop world had moved on, and Jet Harris was 'out' as far as the general public were concerned.

For the next few years, Jet continued to lead a dysfunctional life characterised by frequent moves, casual jobs to earn rent and drink money, and unsuccessful attempts to get back into the music business.

On 11 September 1968, the *Daily Express* reported that Jet had been remanded on bail the day before, having been found 'slumped over the steering wheel of a stationary mini-car in Marylebone. A blood sample taken after his arrest showed that he had 313 milligrams of alcohol – nearly four times over the permitted level... Harris of Porchester Terrace, Paddington pleaded guilty to being in charge of the car, but not driving while unfit through drink or drugs.'

Described by the police as 'a very, very heavy drinker', Jet also admitted unauthorised possession of a small quantity of cannabis resin and LSD and was further remanded on bail of £100 until 26 September. He subsequently received a five-month jail sentence suspended for three years, a three-year driving ban, and a fine of £70 with seven guineas costs.

1969 found Jet working as a barman on the Sussex coast, where he met a girl called Anne Fraschetti. It appears that the relationship was serious, but short-lived. Alcohol again. He is also known to have worked on a building site and at a dog-training school during that year, but compared to his former show-business success his life was going nowhere.

The chance arrival of a royalty cheque in October 1970 would change all that. With his new-found wealth, Jet decided to treat himself to a fortnight's holiday in Jersey.

It was in the Jersey sunshine that his luck changed for the better when he met Margaret Johnston, an attractive young Scots girl who was a qualified nurse doing her RGN at St Helier General Hospital. Maggie had had something of a sheltered upbringing, and amazingly had never even heard of the Shadows, let alone the 'mean, moody and magnificent' Jet Harris. Her looks, and the fact that she liked him for who he was – plain Terry Harris – seems to be what attracted Jet to her.

Not that Jet could stay incognito for long. The owner of

the Jubilee Hotel in St Helier was a fan, and offered him a residency there backing a singer/guitarist called Paul Wagner.

A few months later, Jet and Maggie got a flat together – which is when the problems began to surface. Maggie was in love with Jet, but although he gamely tried his hand at a variety of jobs including cockle-picking, cooking and hospital portering, his drinking continued. If she tried to stop him, he became angry. After one such row turned into physical violence, she reported him to the authorities. As a result, Jet was sectioned into a psychiatric ward at St Helier Hospital for six weeks.

They were reconciled, but the drinking and occasional violence, triggered by her intervention, continued. Eventually, Maggie could take no more and applied for a midwifery course in Cheltenham. She left the island in 1974.

Cheltenham & Gloucester

One week after arriving in Cheltenham, Maggie received a letter from Jet informing her that he was now also living in the town and working as a bus conductor! His persistence paid off. Maggie decided to give him one more chance, but only on condition that he stayed sober. Incredibly, he managed to keep it up for a year – though she had her work cut out to make sure he didn't go off the rails.

They married on 5 April 1975 in Cheltenham, shortly after Maggie finished her training, and moved to Little Witcombe near Gloucester. They had three children, Ben (born 1976), Sam (1980) and Craig (1986), and enjoyed a reasonably settled family life – on and off. According to Maggie, Jet managed to stay sober for two years at one point. In the early '80s, he found employment building fruit machines for Marian Electronics in Chalford (and later Briscombe), then took up professional photography (a skill he'd picked up from Dezo Hoffman back in his Shadows days), specialising in wildlife and industrial images. Jet was acknowledged to be an excellent photographer and at one point was invited to exhibit some of his work at Cheltenham Art Gallery.

But the lure of show business – and the booze that went with it – was never far away. In mid-1975, he was contacted by

Roger LaVern, former organist of the Tornados, who was interested in managing him:

'I didn't have his address, so I travelled up to Gloucester and went to the police station to see if they knew where he was staying. The police usually know all the 'faces' in their area. I found him living in a caravan in a field in Little Witcombe – it was on a caravan site. He was shocked to see me. At the time, he was drinking a lot and not working.

'I took him to London and bought him a guitar. We went to Nathaniel Berry's on Holloway Road, and I told him he could pick any guitar in the shop – no limit on price.'

Upon his return, Jet put a group together with himself on lead, Jimmy Sloane on rhythm guitar, Gordon Wood on bass and Ken Newman on drums,

'I also bought equipment for the rest of the group. They rehearsed in a pub in Little Witcombe, or close by in the area.

'I wanted Jet to record a tune I'd written called 'Theme For A Fallen Idol', so I set up a session at Regent Sound in Denmark Street. I lined up some violinists and a pianist, had scores written for them, put everything in place. In the evening before the session, I went down to Paddington Station to meet Jet.

'When I arrived, there was a commotion going on. It was Jet, shouting and singing at the top of his voice. He'd been drinking before he set off, and drinking on the train, and he was in a right state.

'In the taxi on the way to the studio, Jet said, "I want some fags!" We stopped outside this pub in Albany Street and I said, "You wait here, I'll go and get you some." As I was standing at the bar, I heard something going on behind me. Jet had, in his drunken state, sneaked in after me, gone over to a group of blokes who were sitting there drinking and took a big swig out of this man's pint! That, of course, is a declaration of war in any language – any country! I quickly went over and gave them some money to buy another round, and got him out of there – 'fast' is not the word for it!

'I'd booked Jet into a small hotel at Crouch End, near where I was living at the time. On the way there, after the incident at the pub, Jet said he was "peckish for nosh". So, we stopped off at a Chinese restaurant for something to eat. While we were waiting to be served, Jet got up and helped himself to a huge king prawn off the plate of a man who was sitting across from us! And so, I ended up having to pay for his meal as well. When we got to the hotel, Jet screamed at me because the hotel didn't have a bar. What an evening!

'The session itself was a complete washout. Jet, still hung over from the previous night's drinking, was so drunk he was unable to play, and in the end we just got the violinists and pianist to lay down a backing track – a total waste of studio time and my money.

A few weeks after that, I got Mick Abrahams, who had played with Jethro Tull and Blodwyn Pig, to add the lead guitar part to the backing track. We did that in a studio in Pinner, Middlesex. I said to him, "Play like a prat – nothing clever. OK? Just play the top line straight." He managed to restrain himself until the fade-out, then he threw in some real Mick Abrahams fancy stuff. So, for years I've had people saying to me, "That wasn't really Jet Harris playing on there, was it?"

'It came out on SRT Records in October 1975 with 'This Sportin' Life' on the flip. That was recorded on another occasion, and Jet did play on it. 'Theme For A Fallen Idol' was later reissued as 'Theme' *b/w* 'The Guitar Man', which I also wrote, although I gave Jet half of the credit. That one we cut in a studio in Wetherby in Yorkshire.

'Around the same time as the single came out, I managed to get Jet on a couple of TV shows, including *Take Two*, Thames TV's late-night chat show hosted by Sandra Harris and Llew Gardner. That week's theme was about people who'd had money and had lost money, so it fitted Jet perfectly. Jess Conrad was also there on the show.

'They put us in the hospitality suite before the show, and the inevitable happened. Jet started drinking, and when I tried to get him to ease off, he became abusive and cursed me out in front of everyone. I felt embarrassed and belittled.

'He went on the show completely drunk. He ignored the presenter: instead of answering her questions, he leant over to the side and had a conversation with Jess Conrad. The programme went out live, so there was nothing I could do. It was a disaster. The next day, my phone didn't stop ringing. Everybody was cancelling shows: "Sorry, Roger, but we just can't take the risk of booking Jet."

'I did get him a few bookings at Dingwall's in Camden Town, but on the proviso that he didn't drink before going on. I did a deal with him: "Jet, you do your bit on stage. Afterwards, I will buy all the drinks." That's how we got through it.'

In 1976, Jet persuaded Jim Budd, landlord of the Red Lion in Gloucester, to let him rehearse at his pub. Budd was not impressed with what he heard: 'I told Jet bluntly that his band was a load of shit! The line-up was wrong, and Jet was getting more tense and frustrated. The only member of the group who truly seemed right was Kenny Newman, the drummer. If Jet was to ride another crest, he would have to return to bass, get a respectable lead guitar in, and start using quality equipment.' Exit Messrs Sloane and Wood; enter lead guitarist Laurel Jones and rhythm guitarist Graham Sayce.

By now, Jet's relationship with Roger LaVern had also started to deteriorate, as Budd recalls: 'I don't think Jet came to dislike Roger LaVern, it was just that LaVern was the first person in years to put pressure on Jet to develop some self-discipline and responsibility, and Jet was just not up to it. He became a bag of nerves if a visit from LaVern was pending, and was reduced to asking me to open the letters that LaVern wrote to him and read them to him.'

Eventually, LaVern decided to call time: 'My business relationship with Jet ended in the summer of 1976. I'd had enough! I hired a van and went up with a mate to the pub in Gloucestershire near Jet's home where the band used to rehearse and reclaimed all the gear. He was very unhappy about that, but it was my property, after all. I later heard that he'd traded the guitar I bought him for a drink. The whole sorry episode with Jet Harris left me out of pocket. Absolutely no use suing him – because he had nothing!'

Jim Budd quickly stepped into the breach, bought new

equipment for the band (who at Laurel Jones's suggestion named themselves 'The Diamonds') and set about booking some club dates for them. Despite the fact that Harris and Jones were both chronic alcoholics, the group managed to achieve a degree of success, including a high-profile appearance at the *Edinburgh Festival*. Even so, he later remarked, 'Had I known then what I was going into, I swear I would have sold the pub and entered a monastery!'

His biggest achievement, however, was producing Jet's first solo LP. Inspired perhaps by the success of Johnny Cash's *San Quentin* album, he contacted the chaplain at Gloucester Prison and arranged a concert for the inmates on 3 April 1977 in the prison chapel. Without telling anyone, Budd hid a tape machine under his chair and recorded the entire proceedings – with surprisingly good results.

After editing and mastering by Howard Powell at the small Fleetwood Studios in Stroud, Jet's 'prison' recordings were eventually released in February 1978 on the Ellie Jay label as *Inside Jet Harris*. The atmospheric live set captured the band in their element, running through a selection of Shadows hits and other instrumentals with a studied ease, good sound and just the right amount of echo. In between the numbers, Jet can be heard exchanging good-natured banter with the prisoners: 'Anybody know where the bar is?', 'Could you possibly get me one of those shirts?', etc.

The first he or the group knew about the record was when Jim Budd walked in with a copy. 'He came up to me like a proud father and showed me a finished album,' Jet later recalled. 'If we'd known about it, we'd have done a better job!'

However, not everyone was happy. Lead guitarist Laurel Jones and the other Diamonds took exception to the fact that they were not mentioned anywhere on the LP, and there were the inevitable arguments about money. The group broke up shortly after, leaving Jet stranded (though he has since played with various 'Diamonds' line-ups led by Jones over the years).

A poignant moment for Jet came in March 1978, when Cliff Richard and the Shadows reunited on stage for the first time

Jet in the mid-'80s.

in ten years at the London Palladium. Jet was not invited.

In their 3 March edition, the *Daily Express* ran a rather sad, introspective piece entitled A PALE SHADOW:

'Tonight Cliff Richard and the "old" Shadows will step onto the stage at the London Palladium, but Terence 'Jet' Harris will not be there. Instead, he will be at his terraced house on the outskirts of Gloucester looking after his children while his wife

Maggie goes to her work as a night nurse at an old folks' home. The once-bleached hair is ginger and thinning.

'"My God, I'd give anything to be at the Palladium," said the former Shadow. "If only they'd asked me... I'd have given a damned good show."

'"I'm not strong enough to go out and face an audience by myself," he told me as he rolled a cigarette. "But that's the trouble – people want me to go out and be 'Jet Harris'."

'It is nine years since Harris last saw Cliff Richard or any of the other Shadows. It has been a long distressing fall for a man whose records...sold in millions. Harris, 39, has worked as a gravedigger, potato planter, trawlerman, second chef, brickie and hospital porter. His last job was "on the buses" and that was three years ago. "I destroyed myself," he said. "Booze – my God, the booze. And birds."'

Jet was clearly not in a good frame of mind at this point in his life, and the bottle was never far away. Remaining copies of the *Inside* LP were duly remarketed as *'The Last Concert'* with a footnote from Jim Budd on the back cover explaining that 'Jet's health could take no more and he ceased performing'. Apart from a brief spell with the revival band, Vintage, he seems to have stayed out of music for the next few years. The 'prison' album, however, has stood the test of time and has since been reissued twice on CD.

In 1982, Carol Costa sold her story to the *Daily Star*. The revelations about her secret affair with Cliff came as a bombshell to his disbelieving fans. In 2008's *Cliff Richard, The Bachelor Boy*, Carol explained that she had been approached by Jet and Tony Meehan with a view to them collectively writing something nice about Cliff. However, when it transpired that they were intending to make out that the singer was gay, she told them she would have no part of it and subsequently decided to go public to quash any such rumours.

The mid-'80s found Jet back on the music scene again in a small way. He played with the Strangers (one concert was issued on cassette as *Live In '85* by his UK fan club) and toured Norway, Sweden and the Netherlands. In 1985, he was also tempted back into the studio to guest on a single on the Official Records label by singer/songwriter Peter Rawes, playing bowed double bass on 'Why Should I Ask Her To Stay' and electric bass guitar on the flip, 'Theme From Sharks'.

As 1985 drew to a close, Maggie discovered that her husband was having an affair with a woman he had met during one of his drying-out spells in hospital. That was the final straw for the marriage and Jet got his marching orders. Maggie was left caring for their two young boys while eight months pregnant with their third. Although she did see him again from time to time, he effectively absolved himself of any responsibility for his family from this point. There was to be no reconciliation.

Jet now redoubled his efforts to get back into show business. The new lady in his life, Jackie Bassett, acted as his manager and from their business stationery (headed *'Jet & Jackie Harris'*) it is clear that they regarded themselves as a couple.

Jackie seems to have done a great deal to help resurrect Jet's career, getting him back in the studio in 1988 to re-cut all his classics for an *Anniversary Album* (released on LP and CD) and spin-off single, and organising a video release of a live gig he played at Weston-super-Mare with Bristol group Tangent.

In 1989, Cliff Richard organised *The Event*, a celebration of his 30th anniversary in the business. It was staged at London's Wembley Stadium on 16 and 17 June, and attracted a sell-out crowd of 70,000 on both days. As a result of Hank and Bruce declining to appear in the *Oh Boy!* segment of the show, Jet was invited by Cliff to take part and was happy to do so (he joined Tony Meehan on stage for a memorable rendition of 'Move It'). He wrote off the past concerning Cliff and Carol, saying that they were all just children back then, and went on to say that he was fond of Cliff and grateful for the support he had given him. Jet added: 'To me he's almost St. Cliff, he's such a special person.'

Just weeks after *The Event* Jet was in the papers again, this time on account of a fling he'd allegedly had with Donna Webb, Cliff's oldest sister.

The Comeback

Jet's relationship with Jackie ended in the early 1990s and his drinking went on unchecked. He ended up living with his mother at her home in Upton St Leonards, where she'd recently moved to following the death of his father. He stayed there for five or six years and made further sporadic attempts to get back into the business, playing with different groups and recording with the Rapiers and Tangent (documented by the 1994 album, *Together*).

On 25 November 1995 Jet went to Bournemouth International Conference Centre to see Hank Marvin perform. While he was sitting in the bar, a 35-year-old catering supervisor called Janet Fletcher came over for a chat. They hit it off immediately and a romance quickly blossomed.

At the start of 1996, the couple took a flat together in Gloucester, initially living on welfare payments, most of which Jet squandered on drink. It was a miserable existence, and not at all the sort of future Janet had hoped for. Not only that, years of alcohol abuse were by now starting to seriously impact on Jet's health.

He was now playing as an occasional member of Barry Gibson's Local Heroes (featuring 'honorary' Shadows Alan Jones and Cliff Hall on bass and keyboards, ex-Tornado Clem Cattini on drums, and Barry Gibson and Phil Kelly on guitars), and it was thanks to Gibson's intervention that help came three or four months later.

Barry contacted the famous psychologist and long-time Shadows fan Amedeo Maffei, who offered Jet a free course of treatment for his alcoholism at his clinic in Sirtori, northern Italy, as a 'thank you' for the pleasure his music had given him. Apart from two brief relapses, the cure ultimately proved successful and probably saved Jet's life.

On 23 December 1996, Jet and Janet were married at Gloucester Registry Office. Interviewed by the *Daily Mail*, Jet confided: 'I'm a great believer in fate, and I know Janet and I were meant to be. Now I'm working harder than ever to get it right. Not everyone gets another chance. I'm not going to blow it this time.'

He now set about rebuilding his career in earnest. In 1997, Jet guested on a couple of tracks on the Local Heroes' tribute album, *One Of Our Shadows Is Missing*, and also shared a CD compilation with Alan Jones (bass player with the Shadows from 1977 until 1988, when a horrific motorway crash put him out of action for several years) called *Two Of A Kind*.

Jet toured with Billie Davis in 1998 and recorded a fast-paced duet with her called 'Back In Our Rock'n'Roll Days', which was issued as a CD single. In the same year he was presented with a Fender Lifetime Achievement Award for his role in popularising the bass guitar in Britain. He also appeared at the very first *Shadowmania* and went on to be a regular attender at the annual get-together organised by Bruce Welch.

On 10 July 1999, Jet marked his 60th birthday with a celebration concert with Shadoogie and former Shadows' keyboard player (1978-90), Cliff Hall. The entire show was recorded and released the following year by his British fan club.

October 1999 witnessed the release of *The Phoenix Rises*, which many fans regard as Jet's official 'comeback' album.

On 21 November, he made an unannounced appearance onstage with Hank Marvin at the Birmingham NEC. It was the first time the two men had performed together in 37 years. When they played 'Nivram', 'Kon-Tiki' and 'Apache', it was reported that there were tears in the eyes of many of those present. Future appearances together were mooted, but sadly never materialised.

With the drink out of the way and Janet taking care of business, the bookings started to come in again. Personal appearances in the UK, Ireland, France, Germany, Norway and the Netherlands, and two TV documentaries, *From The Edge: Skint* (1999) and *After They Were Famous* (2000), helped to build up Jet's public profile.

In 2000, Jet and Janet decided to settle on the Isle of Wight. A 70-minute video of a memorable concert with the Rapiers, *Live At The Isle of Wight*, followed soon after, and his revived career continued to make encouraging progress. Over the next couple of years, he appeared with the Rapiers, Mike Berry &

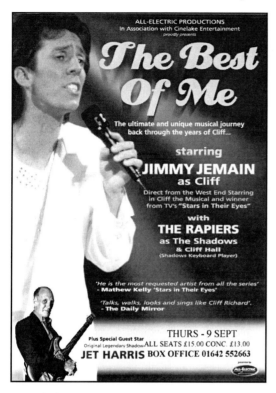

The Outlaws, Clem Cattini & The Tornados and the Bobby Graham Rock Experience. Legendary session drummer Graham also joined him on his new CD, *Diamonds Are Trumps*, released in 2002.

On 9 March 2003, Jet topped the bill at a special *Stars Of The '60s* concert at the London Palladium, which also featured the Rapiers (as Harris's 'Shadows'), John Leyton, the Spotnicks, the Tornados, Mike Berry and Johnny & The Hurricanes.

In 2004, Jet was a special guest star on a touring Cliff Richard tribute show, *The Best Of Me*, starring Cliff impersonator Jimmy Jemain. Some fans who saw the show thought Jet looked nervous, and that the backing group carried him through in places. On his own shows, however, he seemed to have come to terms with his lifelong stage nerves, and his concerts had an intimate quality as he drew the audience into his life and entertained them with his line in self-deprecating humour – for example about his baldness: 'I spent twenty minutes tonight combing my hair, and I've left the bugger in the dressing room!'

The public love to think that their idols suffer with the same problems as they do: it creates a feeling of shared identity and, crucially, a bond. Some older artists who are sensitive about the ravages of time to their once glamorous image, or their failing powers in stage performance, often use bonding ploys to get the audience onside from the beginning. It makes sense to joke about your own weaknesses and get the audience laughing at your expense – but *with* you rather than at you.

Jet on stage, 2004.

Before and after shows, Jet took time out to talk to fans, whether they bought his merchandise or not, and patiently indulged autograph-hunting anoraks, some of whom may have brought dozens of items to be signed, but never dreamt of paying to see his show. Certainly, his loyal band of fans, many of who had kept the flame going for over half a century, regarded him as 'good old Jet' – the star with the common touch.

In 2006, Jet released his first solo single for several decades, 'San Antonio'. His marriage to Janet Fletcher fell apart in 2007, but within months he was back in the papers proudly announcing a new lady in his life, Janet Hemingway, and promoting his latest CD, *The Journey.*

Although he had little hope of recapturing his past success, Jet had come a long way since giving up drink over a decade ago. He had now re-established his credibility within the music business, often performing with old friends like Billie Davis and recording regularly, and seemed able to cope with life's problems without having to resort to the bottle for courage or comfort.

Sadly, Jet's run of good fortune ran out at the end of 2008. The first blow came when Cliff and the Shadows announced that they were going to re-form for a *Final Reunion Tour* in September/October 2009 to mark their 50th anniversary. Again, as in 1978, Jet was not invited.

In the *Daily Mail* of 6 December 2008, he complained: 'Surely it's obvious that I should be there as one of the original members of the Shadows. This is supposed to be a bit of history. I even named the band! They will surely be playing the early songs which I put my stamp on. I think a lot of fans will frown at this. I could have done a cameo at least. But no one has called to explain why... I'm not going to throw a wobbly. There's no malice there. They know my number if they want to get in touch.'

Despite his protestations, and an outcry from fans and some fellow artists (among them Keith Richards, who wrote: 'Jet is an absolute music legend! He deserves a spot of at least 30 minutes banging out the songs he played on! I am going to the tour, but it will be a travesty if he is not there!'), Jet never got the phone call.

Jet Harris

50TH ANNIVERSARY TOUR

SPECIAL GUEST MISS BILLIE DAVIS

THE VICTORIA THEATRE HALIFAX

SEPTEMBER 24th 7.30pm
BOX OFFICE 01422-351158. £18.00.
www.victoriatheatre.co.uk

Sir Cliff's spokesman, Bill Latham explained: 'There's no reason, other than the fact that Jet had left the group in the early days. He was one of the originals, but the line-up has changed a lot since then. Mark Griffiths has played *[bass]* with the Shadows many times.'

True, the Shadows had existed for fifty years, but out of that time Jet had only been a member for less than four of them. Plus the shows were destined to be sell-outs regardless of whether he played or not. There was also a feeling in some quarters that, with the best will in the world, he may not have been up to the demands of sustained professional playing at the very highest level perfected by Messrs Marvin, Welch and Bennett over a showbiz lifetime. Even so, a guest spot for him at a couple of the London gigs would have been a significant gesture: recognition for his contribution to some of their earliest hits and the phenomenal success that followed.

Undaunted, Jet unveiled plans for his own alternative *50th Anniversary Tour* in the autumn with 'special guest Miss Billie Davis'. Unfortunately, it never happened. Shortly after he'd celebrated his 70th birthday in July 2009, it was announced that he was undergoing medical investigations into shoulder pains he'd recently been experiencing.

A statement subsequently appeared on Jet's official website that he had been diagnosed with cancer, was receiving chemotherapy, and had cancelled all appearances until further notice. Bravely, however, he did turn up at one of the cancelled shows – on 21 November at the Warner Bembridge Coast Hotel, near to his home on the Isle of Wight – and joined the Rapiers on stage for two numbers. Appreciative fans gave him a standing ovation.

But the old warrior came back to enjoy a very late Indian summer. Finally recognised for his contribution to UK music, Jet was awarded the MBE in the 2010 New Year's Honours List. Whilst continuing his treatment, he made occasional appearances between March and July with old friends John Leyton and Mike Berry. In October and November, Jet joined Marty Wilde and Eden Kane on a nationwide Flying Music tour and was very well received, with many fans saying they hadn't seen him play so well in years.

Sadly, this exhausting *Born To Rock'n'Roll* tour was to be his last major hurrah. Although he managed some more appearances in the early months of 2011, Jet finally succumbed to cancer at the age of 71. He died in the early hours of 18 March in Winchester at the home of his partner, Janet Hemingway.

THE
INTERVIEWS

Mike Berry

PERFORMER

The first time I met Jet Harris was in 1963 when I was on a Robert Stigwood *'All Stars'* tour with my group, the Innocents. John Leyton was the headliner and other acts included Jet & Tony and Mike Sarne and Billie Davis. Jet chased after Billie, who was getting a lift from Mike Sarne. I don't know whether he had a crash as a result, but at this time it was clear that he had a bad drink problem.

I was never overawed by anybody in the business, and when we first met up with Jet he told us that 'Scarlett O'Hara' had gone to No.2 in the UK charts. We didn't react to his news and so he said, a bit peevishly, 'Cor blimey! Have I got to tour with you bloody lot?'

In the '80s, I met Jet again when I worked with Chris Black & Black Cat and other solo artists like Tommy Bruce, Wee Willie Harris, Ricky Valance and Cliff Bennett. Chris Black was the promoter, guitarist, and provided the band: he did it all.

After that, we didn't meet up again until the mid-to-late '90s when a Portsmouth promoter, David Strand, contacted me and many other '60s acts for a series of concerts and Jet was on the bill with his group, the Rapiers.

David was a big Jet Harris fan and he told Jet, 'I'm going to put you back where you belong.' He had this big stretch limousine for Jet to come to the gigs. I don't think Jet would get into it, so David used it himself: he fancied himself as a bit of a star. When he came to the first gig he had all this jewellery on and young women with big bouffant hairdos.

Looking after artists and promoting is a 24-hour-a-day job, but although David meant well he wasn't very experienced and a bit of a dreamer. This is a hard business and he didn't have the knowledge of how things worked. The crunch came when he realised that it wasn't as easy as he thought it would be. It all got out of hand, and in the end he had to start pulling gigs that he couldn't afford to put on. He had underestimated the cost and had to pull out, and that's when Jet and I tried to salvage something. So, I decided to have a go myself and managed to save a few of them, but had to admit defeat after a good try which involved mailing 200 theatres and getting six replies.

After that, I teamed up with Jet again through his current agent, Vic Farrow, and it was at this time that I got to know him better. Jet, who is now totally sober, is a very honest bloke who has a great sense of humour. In the business he has done it all and been through so much. But he has survived, come back, and is still topping bills over forty years after his first success. Audiences love him, not only for his playing, which is so distinctive, but because of his dry, self-mocking humour which today is a great bonus on his shows. He is a musical legend and nearly everybody – with the exception of the very young – has heard of Jet Harris, and millions of people would love to have been him and lived that legend.

Tommy Bruce

PERFORMER

I have known Jet for more than forty years and always enjoy time spent in his company. He is a great mate, and although we do not see each other as much as we did, I always think of the times we worked together.

He is a very generous man, and even though we have not gigged together for a while, I have followed him into venues. If this involves overnight accommodation, I can guarantee finding a note from Jet telling me to have a good show and leaving me bread, milk and toilet paper. These things were very often in short supply when we toured in the '60s.

I look forward to reading his book so that I can relive many happy memories with him. I have loved to hear Jet play right from the early days with the Shads and then with Tony Meehan on recordings like 'Diamonds' through to the present day. A great bass player!

Keep on rockin', Jet!

Clem Cattini

MUSICIAN

I first came across Jet during the late 1950s in the 2I's, which at that time was the centre of British rock'n'roll. My group then was Terry Kennedy's Rock'n'Rollers, and when I was with them we appeared on a variety bill with the great comedian, Max Wall. He was such a lovely man and gave us all the help we could possibly ask for: like how to present ourselves onstage, what to do and what not to do. And he was so funny! I used to watch him every single night and I was on the floor. After that tour, Paul Lincoln, who managed the 2I's and Terry Dene, asked us if we would like to go out as Terry Dene's backing group, so we became the Dene Aces. Jet was with Terry Dene before I was.

In those days, I knew Jet, but not all that well, and although we were both playing in bands and we did play together on two or three occasions down the 2I's, we weren't mates. I was more friendly with Hank and Bruce: I knew those two better as they used to come to my house before they were the Shadows and my wife used to feed them. Jet came on the scene when the Drifters formed, and they used him on bass.

I remember when Jet was offered the job with the Drifters, he was distraught because he had to have an amplifier and he didn't have one. So I actually went to Selmer's in Charing Cross Road and bought him one brand new. It was quite a big one. He doesn't remember that now, but at the time he was over the moon and so grateful. But I actually bought it, and it cost me £80, which was quite a lot of money in those days. I only did it because he was distraught and I felt sorry for him. If he hadn't got the amplifier, he wouldn't have got the job. Jet was a good player and one of the first to play the electric bass guitar. It was quite a few years later, but Jet did pay me back for that amp. Our paths hadn't really crossed much, as Jet was working with the

Drifters/Shadows and I was working with the Dene Aces and later the Tornados.

However, we did a show with Cliff & The Drifters at the Trocadero, Elephant & Castle, before 'Apache' came along. I cannot remember who else was on the bill, but they got everything thrown at them: ashtrays, cartons – everything. The Teddy boys got narked at Cliff 'cause their girlfriends were screaming at him. Rock'n'roll, when it first started, was really a guys' thing. When we were with Terry Kennedy's Rock'n'Rollers – with Max Wall – the lads loved us: we were like idols and went down a storm. In fairness, they wouldn't have been coming to see Max Wall. In fact, they used to boo him.

Jet and I never kept in touch over the years, but our paths crossed the odd time. After the Shadows and Jet & Tony, I'd heard that he was on the buses and knew he was a good photographer, and then suddenly he's back in rock'n'roll. I've only got to know Jet better in the last ten years when I've worked with the Tornados and we've been on the same show. Now, we speak on the phone from time to time, as well as the shows.

We've actually backed him as well. I was with the Local Heroes and we went to Holland for one of those Cliff Richard/ Shadows things, and that's when I really got to know Jet, because he was out there with us doing his own stuff.

It's funny, but one year we got invited to one of those Shadows conventions as *'The Tornados – Special Guests'*. Of course, our music was totally different anyway, and we certainly didn't play 'Apache'! At the end of our set, some guy came up to us and thanked us for being different, as he couldn't stand to hear another band play 'Apache'. I must admit I've got a passionate hate of tribute bands. When we go on tour as the Tornados, we do stuff that other groups and singers have done, but we don't call ourselves by the original artists' names. The artists who make their living off tribute bands haven't got the talent to make it on their own, so they've got to borrow somebody else's talent and name to make a living for themselves.

Terry's great now, but to be honest, in the beginning he was an arse when he was drunk – and aggressive with it. I didn't have a lot of respect for him when he was with the Shadows, obviously because of the way that he was. Presumably he behaved like that with everyone.

One of the show business meeting places was the Lotus House restaurant in the Edgware Road. The Tornados had just got to the top of the charts and suddenly I had a bit of money, so I decided to take my wife out for dinner, and the Shadows were in there at the time. Jet, who was drunk, came up to me, put a pound note in my hand and said, 'Here you are, son, see you later!' I wasn't very happy about that and pulled him about it. I had him up against a wall, and either Bruce or Hank came up and pulled us apart. I shouldn't have reacted like that in front of my wife, but he angered me. But Jet won't remember that incident. He was out of it, so whether he recognised me or not I don't know. He was just acting 'big time' – and the funny thing was he still owed me the £80 for the amplifier! I was so incensed: I thought, *You cheeky sod!*

It's just a revelation what's happened to him and I'm just so pleased for the guy. He's playing great and he's got a great sense of humour. Today I get on very well with Jet. He's more personable, and I've got a lot of respect and a lot of time for him. To give up the alcohol – he's done great as a man to do that, because he did go through a really heavy scene with the drink. Jet's still very nervous before a show, but he's playing great and is very funny with his great sense of humour and line in cockney patter.

Jet didn't set my ears alight as a player, but I'm probably a bit harsh with doing session work. I've probably worked with the finest bass players in England. In fairness, if it hadn't been for the drink taking over the situation, the guy could have been a very, very top player.

Billie Davis

PERFORMER AND JET'S GIRLFRIEND 1963-65

When I was a teenager, Southall Community Centre and Kew Boathouse were the places to go, and one night, at Southall, my best girlfriend, Sue, pushed me up onto the stage for a talent contest. Cliff Bennett was backing me that night and I won the contest. That's how it all started for me. Then I recorded some stuff with the legendary Joe Meek, which is in the famous 'missing trunk'. It contains a lot of unissued masters including two of mine – 'Mr Right' and 'School Is Over' – and a lot of people would like to get a hold of it.

Around 1962 I met Robert Stigwood at Joe Meek's when he was recording John Leyton, and from then on Stigwood became my manager. I was 16 when I signed with him and my grandmother had to sign the contract for me. Robert Stigwood put me through fashion school, drama school and all that stuff before I actually recorded the first comedy record for EMI Parlophone – called 'Will I What?' – with Mike Sarne, who was also managed by Stigwood. Wendy Richard preceded me on the comedy duets with Mike and they had a big hit with 'Come Outside'. Anyway, as a result of this we went out and did various concerts and theatre work for the Stigwood Organisation.

Robert Stigwood had decided that I would have to wait for the right solo record and I went on to do 'Tell Him', which he found in America when he was filming *The Great Escape* with John Leyton. They thought that it would be the most perfect song for me and brought it back with them. I was offered 'The Loco-motion', but I just felt that I couldn't compete with Carole King 'cause she had written it and I adored Carole King's stuff back then anyway.

As a result of that record, I went to do the TV show *Thank Your Lucky Stars* at studios in Birmingham. The Beatles were on that show as well, and here I am sitting watching the rehearsal with these four Scouse lads with funny accents chatting me up and everyone was looking. At that particular time they all seemed to roll on these huge Billy Fury-type sets, because Billy was so big then and he'd do the show every week. And I can remember Ringo saying, 'Look at that. One day we'll be as big as that.' We turned round to see their little drum kit being wheeled onto the set to go on the rostrum, and there they had 'The Beatles' written in cardboard to go behind them.

But the funny thing was that Jet and Tony Meehan were on the same show, and when we'd had a break I'd met Jet in the green room for tea. He said, 'Hello, you're not a fella after all!' I looked at him and thought, *What's he talking about?* Apparently, Tony Meehan had said to him, 'Oh, that new singer called Billie Davis is doing the show with us.' And Jet had said, 'Who's he then?'

Jet had this very photogenic face, and with the blond hair it really stood out. He did have a few acting lessons, but unfortunately he didn't carry on with it. He could have done very well there, but this is where the bottle took over. He was a very sweet, petite man and he always looked as if he should be mothered. He was – and is – funny and witty, and I still think he should be doing stand-up comedy. Nobody knew him quite like I did.

After that Birmingham episode where we met, he asked me if he could call me, which he did. He told me later that he'd had a confrontation with Patti Brook, his girlfriend at that time. I wouldn't say that I was in love with him at first sight, as I was a bit afraid of what this person was all about. Right from the off I was aware of Jet's drink problem. When we first met and he chased me, he would often arrive outside my house in the Portobello Road and I don't know how he got there, he was so drunk in that Volvo sports car of his.

So we met, and of course we then had a tour lined up, although at the time of meeting we didn't know we'd be working on the same tour. It was an absolutely amazing tour: there were the Four Seasons, the Rolling Stones, Duffy Power – who was a great soul singer – and we were all on the road together. I can't remember whether Mike Sarne was on that tour, but I was never romantically involved with Mike at any time. Mike Berry was in there and he usually opened the show.

Some of these Stigwood shows were fabulous bills with six or seven pop acts on them. This was very, very new to me and we'd travel on the coach together. Brian Jones, who was going with my friend and companion, Annie Mitchell, liked to travel with us, but the other Stones travelled together by car. The Ray Charles hit at that time was 'Hit The Road Jack', and our coach driver was called Jack, so we all sat on the coach with Jack and we'd go up the M1 and say, 'Hit the road, Jack.' Jet will tell you that on one occasion we were on the coach and Jack shouted, 'Everybody out, the coach is going up!' So it was 'everybody out', and we were running down the M1 as the coach was about to catch fire.

When we were on tour with the Rolling Stones, we used to play tricks on people in the hotels like waking up singer Billy Boyle by sending him the *Times* newspaper with a cup of tea and some porridge at six o'clock in the morning. We were all in the same hotel all night. It was the Midland Hotel in Manchester and it just went berserk with the partying. After that, nobody touring was allowed to stay in that hotel. We were all bloody mad.

I wasn't a great fan of the Shadows at that particular time because that is not the music I was listening to. I was listening to the early rock'n'roll stuff, and I liked the Rolling Stones at the time. I liked stuff that was original and that's why I loved the stuff that Jet did on his own: I absolutely loved it. It was electrifying.

He had a road manager called Sam Curtis, and the presentation alone of Jet & Tony's act was just fantastic: I loved it. When he went onstage and opened up his act with 'The Man With The Golden Arm', they had an effect where you had the lights out, you had Jet's pants and shirt gleaming white – they had a fluorescent paint on his shoes, round his guitar, and on the drums and drumsticks. So you had this fantastic image when he played the opening notes – *da-da-da-da-da* – on his bass guitar. Sam came up with that. He was wonderful and really, really looked after Jet. Sam battled hard to keep him on the straight and narrow by locking him in his dressing room and keeping him away from the bottle and well-wishers who, ignorant of Jet's problem, wanted to buy him drinks.

I have always felt that the band members that Jet had then – the jazzers, the John McLaughlins, the Joe Morettis – were the best, but unfortunately they are no longer with us. The live music was great, but of course in between all this there was always a fight, and we'd have to lock Jet in the dressing rooms because of his nerves and the drink. Of course, he used to climb out of the windows. The doctor we had at that point said, 'You know it's a very strange thing, because Judy Garland had the same thing that Jet had, in that her nerves were based on a fear that she would swallow her tongue.'

For me, the John Leytons and Mike Sarnes of this world, who were actors and all part of the Joe Meek stable, couldn't understand what was going on. And to them it was just a big problem, because this guy was drunk and going onstage. One minute he was fine, and the next minute he was swaying all over the place. We were all under the Robert Stigwood Organisation and we thought that maybe they would kill the show because of the complaints from the public. Tony Meehan had a terrible time to hold Jet together, and then I came on the scene and I shared that problem. And I did try and keep him very, very much together.

I can't remember exactly when we started to live together, but we set up in a flat in Marble Arch at 77 Portsea Hall, which was above the Lotus House Chinese restaurant in Edgware Road. It was a joint rental and I was on a small retainer from Robert Stigwood. And that was when Jet said to me, 'Where's your money going?' I went into the office and asked, 'Well, what's actually happening here? Where's my money?' And that's when I left Robert Stigwood.

Admittedly, Stigwood had paid for my drama and fashion schools and everything, but I was still earning and wanted my money. Then I went to Keith Devon at the Bernard Delfont Organisation, who was Jet's agent. Keith was a lovely man, but we used to sit in his office for ages. Now, Keith had booked Laurel & Hardy for their UK tours, and he was so proud of this that he had their photos all over his office. To amuse ourselves during our long waits, Jet and I used to nick his photos and move them around and then say, 'Hey, how about us!?'

From the time I met Jet, I never knew him sober. I never actually knew him sober. When I first met him, he confided to me almost straightaway that he had begun his drinking over his wife Carol and his boss Cliff Richard, who he suspected were having an affair. He took me down to meet Jack, the landlord of the Marlborough Head pub opposite the London Palladium. Jet used to confide in Jack during his frequent visits to the pub during the *Stars In Your Eyes* six-month Palladium season that he did with Cliff Richard and the rest of the Shadows in 1960. Sometimes they were playing three shows a day. Jet knew that something was going on with his wife and his boss. He told me, 'I couldn't do a thing about it, he was my boss.' Having spoken to Jack myself, I really do think that it was at this stage the trouble really started with the drink. When I came on the scene, he told me that he wasn't divorced from Carol, but I never met her.

The horrendous thing was, of course, the car accident. And that was the time when it all came out in the open, because Jet was a married man and he was having an affair with a young singer – which was me – and it hit the tabloids. That particular evening, I was doing a gig in Evesham in Worcestershire. Jet had picked up an *NME* award that day, and came round to see me and said, 'Come on, I'll come with you. I'll get a car with a driver and we'll go to your gig.' So we did. It was on Saturday, 28 September 1963. The gig was great. We were well up: he was No.1, and I was No.10 in the charts. Coming home in the back of the car we were very tired and sleepy.

A Midland Red bus suddenly pulled out into the road and our car went into it. Jet fell forward and hit his head on the ashtray, and I fell – I had been sleeping sideways – and broke my jaw, although I didn't know this at the time. There was blood everywhere. I got out of the car, carried Jet out, put him on the side of the road. But the lovely thing was – I remember it was

Miss Billie Davis at the Empire Theatre, Consett, 2006.

like a cameo and would make a great film – some fans had been following us from the gig on their scooters and motorbikes and they helped us. I didn't realise at the time, but the strap of the little watch I was wearing had broken in the crash and they must have found it in the wreckage, because the watch was posted to me five or six weeks later. Jet's two *NME* award plaques were in my handbag when we collided and both were badly scratched.

I thought that I was fine and went over to get on the bus for a sit-down, and a little old man was sitting on the bus and had his head bumped when the car crashed into it. I said, 'Are you all right?'

The ambulance man saw me wandering about and said, 'Who are you? What are you doing? Were you on the bus?'

I turned around and said, 'No, I was in the...' And when I turned round and looked at the car, which was a Humber Super Snipe – a really heavy car – I realised that it was a write-off and that I'd been in that car. My knees then went a bit wobbly and he said, 'You'd better get in the ambulance.' Jet and I then went in different directions. He went to the General Hospital, because there was quite a cut on his head and they had to deal with that, and I went to the small hospital. After treatment, Jet discharged himself, came over for me, and we were driven back to London.

We got back, I went to my Marble Arch flat and tried to go to sleep. Suddenly I was woken up by this man who was shaking me and asking where Jet was. I said, 'What are you talking about? Who are you? What do you mean, "Where's Jet?" Go away!'

He said, 'I'm Mike Hellicar from the *Daily Sketch*'. And I realised that I couldn't hardly speak and my face was huge. I asked him to call Robert Stigwood's office for me and ask the PR man to come round, which he did. At that stage I don't think that I knew where Jet was. He was probably drowning his sorrows somewhere. It was all a bit strange, so I went into the London Clinic. For some time afterwards we would visit the Clinic – but in between him going on benders. He wouldn't settle; he should have still been in hospital but he wasn't. He was very, very distressed and I think the build-up to this was his being distraught at the work that he had done at the Palladium and the thing with Cliff and his wife.

I came out of the hospital and the press wouldn't leave us alone. Some friends of ours who were living in Brighton said, 'Look, come down here.' So we went down there, but the press found us. We had to come back to London every so often anyway to see the doctors. My jaw was wired, so I couldn't sing. I couldn't do anything, and I lived on baby foods.

I can remember getting on this train with Jet. We were so naïve, even at that stage. Getting off at Victoria Station, I remember looking up the platform and seeing all these photographers. I looked at my girlfriend Annie and her boyfriend, who were looking after us and who had the apartment in Brighton, and said, 'There's somebody really important on this train.' And of course it was us! A tabloid journalist wrote an article, THE COUPLE WHO CAUGHT THE 10.25, or something like that.

I found a policeman and said, 'Can you get us a cab quickly?' We then went to Harley Street and, when we came out, Dr Meyer, who also treated Judy Garland and Alma Cogan, told the press, 'Go away; leave the kids alone, let them rest. They're ill: they've had an accident.' The doctors told Jet, 'Look you've had injections, but by the time you catch the train and get back to Brighton, you'll be ready to sleep.' We get in the cab, we have all the press around us and we miss the train. Of course, it hits the tabloids that Jet Harris was drunk on Victoria Station – but he was not drunk, he was *drugged*: he's had an injection. We're on the nine o'clock news and all of that.

I did see a future with Jet, but had no idea how bad it was going to be with the drinking. After the accident, he just went to pieces. As a result of the collision, he had a scar on his head, but I think it was more the psychological thing and the drink that pushed him over. The accident was simply the final straw that really triggered everything and brought on his breakdown.

Obviously, I thought that I could cure his drink problem: it was a situation of two people together helping one another. I would arrive home and sometimes he would say, 'I'm going out for a paper,' and three days later he would come back, and of course I didn't know where he was. Jet had a lot of people who knew who he was and were hangers-on. He'd disappear to the pub to drown his sorrows, and suddenly he'd phoned the accountant, got his money and blew it.

Meanwhile I was stuck at home trying to recuperate and get myself together, so that was a very, very hard time. And all of a sudden I was dubbed 'the scarlet lady of pop' because I was going out with a married man, which in those days wasn't good. It didn't seem to matter that Jet's marriage to Carol was over, or there had been others before me. That, and the results of the accident, ruined my career and put me out of action for a long time anyway. And at that time along came Sandie Shaw, along came Lulu, and along came everyone – all sporting the Billie Davis bob!

I was brought up by my grandmother and didn't have a family to turn to, but I tried very hard with Jet's father to say, 'Look, he's very ill, please, the only way is to sign him into somewhere.' It was a terrible thing to do, but the doctors wanted to do it so that they could cure him. He went into the Priory – they talk about the Priory today, right? People are in and out of it like a nursing home. Jet was the first one to go into the Priory at Roehampton.

So he was in and out of the Priory, which at that time was £1,000 a week. And at one point I said, 'All right, I'll look after you. I will cook, and I will get nurses in here three times a day if you like, if you want to stay here in Marble Arch,' and that's what we did. So really, my career went out of the window for that reason. I cared, and I wanted him and I to be married. We'd got engaged after the accident. He wasn't a womaniser when he was with me, and not particularly romantic, but I remember he'd come back one day – these capes were in fashion – and he'd gone out and bought me this lovely yellow cape. We surrounded ourselves with animals and went to the park every day.

Jet was never violent towards me, but he would do things. Like when he came back late to our flat and I'd gone to bed to avoid him being in a drunken state, and if he wanted attention he would slam a door or whatever. He would actually tip me out of bed to get attention. But we did have a minder called Ricky [*Martinez*] and he would actually battle with Jet quite a bit.

Sometimes when I couldn't cope, I would ring his parents and his father would come over and try to help. His dad would be absolutely gutted and tried to talk to him, 'Look son, try and pull yourself together.' Jet hated hospitals, but we had him in and out of hospitals. We had him sedated. We had nurses in and out of the flat – everything to try and help. The doctor had come round one night when he was pretty violent and had been drinking. I used to ring his father, his father would ring the doctor, and the doctor would come round and give him a shot of vitamin B12 or whatever to try and calm him.

One night he got a shot and ended up in some kind of strange hospital ward for the mentally ill in St Pancras. The doctors said that maybe this would teach him a lesson because we had tried every way. The next day I had to go to ATV Studios to record *Ready Steady Go!* and I was sharing a dressing room with Dusty Springfield. Obviously, being the kind of person I am, I was extremely worried about him. So I said to Dusty, who liked Jet anyway, 'Look, could you cover for me while I nip out and go to see him?'

The funny thing was that he was sitting there laughing! He was sharing a ward with other men and they were sitting around in a circle. One guy, to the right of Jet, had been a schoolteacher. His mind had gone, and every time he'd got to the blackboard in a classroom, he forgot his lesson. There was another who had a thing about water so they put him near a tap and he kept filling all these bottles up with water and putting them by the bed. Jet said, 'He's just drunk my orange juice neat 'cause he wants the bottle!' He'd sobered up by this time, so he could appreciate what was going on around him. Really, the trouble was that when Jet drank he became schizophrenic, but when he sobered up he was fine. Another guy had a newspaper and Jet told me that he folded it up into tiny little bits and then he put them all under the ashtrays.

I find all this behaviour very humbling, very sweet and very bizarre, because if you think about it in the right way, it's understandable. I look in the mirror when I've got a problem, scratch my head and say, 'Another fine mess you've got me into, Stanley – again!' But isn't show business like this? One minute you're up; one minute you're down.

Jet's partner, Tony Meehan, was unable to work while Jet was ill, and they were booked to appear on *Ready Steady Go!* As this was the only live show that you could do at that time, it was a very important show and everybody did it. It was broadcast every Friday night. I'm sitting at home watching – there's Cathy McGowan interviewing Tony Meehan, but where's Jet? Suddenly, there's a knock at the door and he comes flying in.

'It's me.'

'What are you doing here?'

'I've run away. I can't cope with anybody. I can't cope with this. I don't want to be pictured, because I don't want people to see this scar on my head.'

It was a large scar, and the thing was that they had shaved his head, so it didn't look very nice and he was very conscious of that. That's when he ran away to Brighton and we stayed there for about six months or more while travelling backwards and forwards to London for treatments, etc. We still had the flat in

Marble Arch, but I can't remember when our relationship finished. When it did, I was front page in the papers: BILLIE – I HAVE LEFT JET. I CAN'T COPE WITH IT ANYMORE. Even then I went back a number of times to try and help him. There were no other women for him at that time, but as I mentioned there were hangers-on, and if there was money around then they'd be there.

I was in love with Jet and it was a proper love affair in the true sense. Jet asked my gran if he could marry me and we were engaged. But unfortunately the whole drunken fiascos which occurred were just too much to cope with. But, you know, when somebody is ill there are some very funny moments, although at the time half of these things weren't funny.

When we lived together in Marble Arch, I had a white poodle which I called Sam, and Jet had an Afghan Hound called Rifka. I had gone out to do an interview because Pye Records was around the corner and we used to do live interviews for Radio Luxembourg there. There were other people there to do interviews, including P.J. Proby, and I got chatting to them. When I got back, he started to question me about who I had been talking to. Now, Jet wasn't really a jealous man – that wasn't his scene – but when he'd had a drink, he could look pretty mean: grit his teeth and that would be it. He had that look, and I think that's why he used to get into trouble in the pubs because it looked like he wanted to fight.

When I'd left the flat that day, Jet was painting the hall a kind of apple-green colour. When I came back, he was still painting the wall, but it was quite clear that he had been to the pub as he was swaying while painting this wall and accusing me of everything. I told him that he didn't know what he was talking about and that I'd just come home from doing these interviews. He decided that he would tip the whole pot of paint over his head. Now, it wasn't a little pot, it was a large two-litre size. Can you imagine? But the funniest things were the dogs: the poodle was running around with a green tail and the Afghan had green on his coat. I put Jet in the bath and cleaned him up, and Jet's father came round when I was doing it. The Afghan was too big for the bath and had to be partially green for a while until we took him to the vet to clip his hair, along with the poodle.

Jet is a wonderful photographer and again that comes into what he's all about: he's a perfectionist. He used to carry a praying mantis around in his pocket and he had some great pictures of it. Unfortunately he sat on it – he was so upset! I still have a picture that Jet took of me in Hyde Park when I was 18 and first met him.

I never knew about all of his pets, but he swears to this day that one of the monkeys he had spoke to him when he was going to sleep one night. It was when he was sharing a room with Hank Marvin, and he woke Hank to tell him, 'Hank, Hank, that monkey has just spoken to me.' And Hank said, 'What do you mean, it's just *spoken* to you?' When Jet went to sleep in those days – he probably still does it – he put his hands up to his face. Well, the monkey used to copy him, and he swears to this day that he was settling down and going to sleep and the monkey who was next to him said, 'Oh, that's lovely.'

Once he came home very late and I was fast asleep, and he drew a face on my bottom! I never knew until I went to have a bath or a shower in the morning and I thought, *What's that on my bottom!?*

At the Marble Arch flat, Jet used to get out of his head with the porter in the lodge downstairs. The doorbell would go and the porter would say to me, 'I've brought Mr Harris up,' and they'd both be swaying at the door. I would grab Jet and pull him in.

We used to have little dinner parties and things, and again this was something that was very funny. This friend of mine remembers the night I was having a dinner party and Jet had gone out and come back, and was falling all over the place drunk and rolling on the floor. And I served the dinner stepping over him. Occasionally he would moan and I would just dig him in the foot or whatever. My guests thought that I was really cruel because he was on the floor and I told him that he should just stay down there.

Sometimes Jet and I would have been somewhere and he'd had so much to drink that we had to pull the car in somewhere so that he could sleep it off. I didn't drive then, and didn't know what to do. That frightened me quite a bit because I was stuck beside this drunk person. Often I had engagements and had to get back to London, but had to wait for him to sober up. I had no one that I could really confide in.

I have a friend, who Jet knows very well, called Brian, and he adores Jet. I can't remember when this was, but it was after the accident when Jet wasn't able to work, wasn't touring, had no money, and was in Brighton. He seemed to love Brighton. Brian would always help Jet out, and on one occasion Jet decided to earn some money in Brighton by window cleaning, and he asked Brian to come down and join him. Brian said, 'Okay, but where am I going to stay?' Jet told him, 'I'll put you up in a hotel, but don't worry about me.' Brian gets down there and they arrange to meet outside a particular pub the next morning at ten o'clock. It's freezing cold weather and Brian is waiting outside this pub. There was a soft-top kiosk that sold cigarettes and things near the pub, and all of a sudden this kiosk opened, and Jet had been sleeping on the top of it! Of course, once Brian had joined him, he would have been the one doing the window cleaning because Jet would be drunk and he'd be swaying up the ladder.

There was some amusement, but it was a constant source of worry. It was the most horrendous thing: you just never knew what was going to happen next. Again, there was a pub called the Duke of Kendal in Marble Arch down the road where we lived. The main door of the pub was jutting out onto the pavement and almost onto the road where two roads forked. One day Jet went down there and they wouldn't let him in because he had been drinking the night before and they had banned him. Jet was furious and drove his jeep down there, backed it up and blew all the exhaust fumes into this pub door. And all the people ran out the other side. Now that was funny! He said, 'I'll teach them,' and that's what he did.

I saw him a long time after our break-up, after his marriage to Susan Speed had ended, and he accompanied me to Denmark where I was singing. He was as drunk as a skunk every night. Years ago, when he was in Gloucester married to Margaret and had young children, I went to see him. They lived across a river, and I was always surprised that he didn't fall into it when he was drunk. I didn't have much back then, but they had absolutely nothing, and I cooked us all a huge pan of spaghetti and looked after them.

I've been sitting here listening to a Lena Horne album, *Lena – Lovely And Alive*, which Jet bought for me, as at the time he was listening to bassist Ray Brown who played with Oscar Peterson. Jet was a jazzer at heart and he taught me to listen. So, I picked up a lot of the Lena Horne stuff and listened to material like that, which I am now doing. What goes around comes around. We've gone full circle here and it's the kind of music Jet should be doing. His technique as a bass player is phenomenal, magical – Jack Good brought that out in him. Personally I think he should be doing things like 'Besame Mucho' and jazzy things. He's not a guitar player; he's a bass player and a lot of people don't realise this unless they really listen. And when he had to switch from bass and do all those guitar things, it wasn't easy for him, he would tell you that. His nerves went and Joe Moretti would often stand in and play for him.

Today, I think his show should be built around him. You could have the girls up front going, 'Hey, everybody...' and turn it into a play covering Tin Pan Alley days and jazz, which he could handle very well. And jazz is coming back again. I've seen it, and I've always seen it, but for some reason it doesn't happen. The whole history of Jet and I would make a great show. But it is a difficult thing. At the end of the day, because he was a bass player with the Shadows, people want to hear the Shadows' numbers and don't look at it any other way.

I didn't really know about Jet's relationships with the other Shadows when he was with them, but I see Bruce Welch through a friend from time to time and when I learned that the Shadows were going back on tour I asked him, 'Why is Jet not on this tour?' He just said, 'I can't take that chance anymore, Billie. I've got so many things planted in my head that have gone wrong, I just can't face it.' Jet used to see the funny side and told me that, for the whole time that he was working with the Shadows, Bruce had a blackhead in his nose and he spent the entire time trying to get it out for him. Jet said that he even tried a steak knife on it, but Bruce said it must have had roots all the way down to his feet!

The thing is with Jet, when I look back on it, he has quite a lot of children knocking about. What I never understood was that he never saw them. He left the women to get on with it. That's sad really, but, having spent a lot of time with Proby – who is not drinking anymore of course – he can't cope with too many people, and Jet's probably the same. But when you drink, the most important thing is the bottle, because you are married to it, aren't you? How can you sum him up? It's so like the Proby situation really – a very talented guy who was married to the bottle. We've always remained friends, but we went through an awful lot together and it would be nice to share those moments again, and perhaps work together.

This business isn't about who's been with who and who did what, etc, and I've never wanted to lift my profile that way. It's not where I'm coming from. People forget all that. It's about the music, your craft. Okay, I met Jet; we fell in love. Terrible things happened like the car accident. Out of that came the revelation of the affair and the whole bit with his wife, him being married and all that stuff. The whole thing was very sad, although a lot of people actually thought that it helped my career! Obviously Stigwood knew what was going on and did look out for me even after I left his management. He did say to me, 'I think this has had an extreme effect on your career.' Robert had his head bolted on properly and managed and recorded acts like the Bee Gees and Cream.

It's amazing when I look back now at all the crazy things that happened. The whole time was quite bizarre and I was very young – really, we were babies – but I try and look at it this way: Jet was ill, he was an alcoholic, and he was drinking to drown his sorrows. I saved his life. I pulled him out of that car, and I nursed him and looked after him very well. We were together for a few years and I left because I just couldn't cope anymore. But out of all of that came the craft side of the business: what we want to do and what we do best. And here I am today: after forty years I'm still standing.

Vince Eager

PERFORMER

I met Jet in early 1958 when I was a resident singer at the 2I's. He came along there and joined in, which other musicians and singers did. He played with Tony Crombie & His Rockets and I did a couple of shows with them. After that, he played for me a few times when I had my own group – Vince Eager & The Vagabonds – at the Churchill Club in London's New Bond Street. Tommy Steele had a very successful run at the Stork Club in London, which was owned by Al Burnett. And Larry Parnes, who was managing me, and being the very clever guy that he was, thought that it would be a good shop window for me, and it proved to be so right. When I knew Jet at this stage, he wasn't drinking and I had no problems with him. Then, I didn't drink at all, so I would have noticed.

At the Churchill there was an 11.00 p.m. supper show and a 1.30 a.m. early breakfast show. We auditioned live in front of ten people at the 11.00 p.m. show, and the club manager, Harry Meadows, asked us to perform in front of a larger audience at the 1.30 a.m. show. We were then signed for a month and that was renewed a further five times.

Later, the Vagabonds were Tony Sheridan, Licorice Locking, Tex Makins and a guy called Rex on slap bass. We left Churchill's because we were given a better-paid contract at Winston's Club by Bruce Brace. He had been the owner of Churchill's, but reluctantly had to sell it to Harry Meadows, so he opened Winston's across the road!

It was at Churchill's that I was auditioned by the *6.5 Special* producer, Russell Turner. Russell really wanted Tommy Steele for the *6.5*, so Larry Parnes gave him one Tommy Steele appearance and thirteen Vince Eager appearances as a package! From *6.5* I went onto *Oh Boy!* twice, but we all lost out when Larry Parnes got into an argument with *Oh Boy!* producer, Jack Good, about what clothes Marty Wilde should wear on the TV show. Marty was No.1 at the time and Cliff was No.2. However, as a result of their dispute, Jack Good wouldn't book any of Larry Parnes's artists from October 1958 to March 1959. In that time, Cliff replaced Marty at No.1 and we all lost out. Jack Good said that had it not been for Larry, Billy Fury would have been bigger than Cliff.

After that, I went onto BBC's *Drumbeat* in 1959 and remember that the Shadows were using new white Strats and Vic Flick and other guitarists were curious and wanted them. Before the white Strat, I think Jet played a Burns.

From the first time I saw Jet, I thought he was going to be a big rock star. He had that James Dean surly, moody look – not nasty, just mean-looking. I think he was a depressive; he didn't smile much, but he was a nice guy to talk to, even though he looked like he had the worries of the world on his shoulders.

As an agent, I booked Jet to headline a big festival in Radcliffe, Nottinghamshire in 2002, and he came with his wife, Janet, and it was a very successful show. It was the first time that we'd seen each other in forty years. After that, I saw him at a charity show for Bobby Graham in Cheshunt, Hertfordshire – Cliff's hometown.

Brian Gregg

MUSICIAN

In 1957, I was in Les Hobeaux and appeared on a bill topped by Larry Page 'the Teenage Rage', and Jet was playing double bass for him. This was at the Playhouse Theatre, Plymouth and was my first professional theatre gig. After that, I joined Colin Hicks & His Cabin Boys before going on to work as a Dene Ace with Terry Dene. Jet also played double bass for Terry, but at a different time. However, he didn't last long as Paul Lincoln told him that he was not up to it. Jet became a good player and you can hear the notes clearly, but his runs are not inventive. That may have changed if he had continued as a jazzer.

As far as I know, a guy in Dickie Bishop's group had the first electric bass guitar in the UK, and he bought it off an American on a US Air Force base in 1956. I'd also seen one in a film featuring Little Richard and his band. I was in Les Hobeaux in those days and saw one in Selmer's window in Charing Cross Road at two o'clock in the morning. I asked Ray Hunter to sign the HP for me. At first he said, 'I'm not signing that for you.' I told him, 'You can take it out of my wages.' But he signed it for me anyway. Barney Smith, who was with Rory Blackwell's rock band, the Blackjacks, had the second bass guitar, as he just beat me to it.

Eric Ford of Lord Rockingham's X1 owned a Selmer and he got me a cello bass and Selmer amp. It was then I met Pepe Rush the electronics wizard, and he fitted me up. Jet was playing a small Vox amp. If you listen to Johnny Kidd & The Pirates, the bass is very aggressive. I was the first player in the UK to feature the electric bass and make it stand out.

I first knew Jet when he became a 2I's person and backed Terry Dene, and Alex Murray and Mickie Most, who were the Most Brothers. When the 2I's closed around 1.00 a.m., we all used to jump in a cab and go for a fry-up to the Ace Café on the

North Circular Road, and we got in with the bikers.

I remember we used to eat at the Lotus House in Edgware Road. On one occasion, Jet was pissed and these guys came in. Jet said, 'Fucking bastards!' and started goading this guy. I told him to fuck off.

It was through me that Jet dyed his hair blond. My wife, Terri, was a singer and dancer and had to have her hair done regularly at Scott's in London's West End. A girl in the hairdresser's gave me a bottle of special powder bleach. I put a bit on the front and then rinsed, and it stuck. Then, I had my whole head blond. I was down Old Compton Street with a suntan and blond hair when I bumped into Jet. He took one look and said, 'That looks fucking great, will you do mine?' We lived in Queensway then, so I took him back to our place and my wife did his hair blond. He added the Vitapointe to give his hair a gloss.

I gave Johnny Foster, Cliff's manager, Jet's phone number, and also told him about Hank and Bruce, who were in the Chesternuts. I was also asked if I wanted to do the Kalin Twins tour with Cliff Richard. I remember the first time I met Cliff: this Pakistani walked in with dark brown hair. He looked like the Indian actor, Sabu – but it was Cliff! The next time I saw Johnny Foster, he was looking for a bass player and I gave him Johnny Booker's phone number to contact Jet.

Although I'm 6'2'', Jet and I used to get confused, as our faces bore a big resemblance and Shadows fans used to come up to me and ask, 'Can I have your autograph?'

During the late 1970s, I was living in Wiltshire and a mate, Adrian, had bumped into Jet and gave him my phone number.

He called me and said, 'Do you remember me?'

I said, 'Of course I remember you, you berk.'

Jet got defensive and said, 'Don't call me a berk!'

I told him it was just a friendly greeting and asked him, 'Do you remember when I got your hair done?'

And Jet said, 'Yes, that's why I went bald!!!'

In the early '80s, I saw him with Margaret and his kids. I said, 'You're a fucking legend.'

He said, 'Don't be silly, I'm not a legend.'

Cliff Hall

MUSICIAN

I first came across Jet when he came to see the Shadows at the NEC, Birmingham in the 1980s. In addition to Hank, Bruce and Brian, Alan Jones was on bass and I was playing keyboards. He brought some fabulous macro photographs of insect and animal life backstage. The reaction from the others was, 'Oh, it's Jet.' He was semi-blanked by them, but he and I hit it off and we went off for a drink somewhere.

Probably drinking caused problems with the other Shadows, but they could have been a little more accommodating to Jet. Shadows fans feel that Jet has been blanked. We all know how they feel and they have made it plain to everybody. At least, with Bruce you always know what he's thinking. He doesn't pull any punches and never has. Hank and Bruce let each other know how they feel. Jet never felt welcome after he left. Bruce Welch knows fans idolise Jet and that he is a big draw – that's why Jet is invited to *Shadowmania*, which in truth is a great social event.

My feelings regarding the Shadows are that I accept they wanted to go in a different direction and use different bass players, and the fans have also had an input. It's a strange thing, but with Alan Jones fans preferred him to Mark Griffiths. The Shadows haven't been musically creative for many years, and over the past five or six years I've pleaded with them to do different tracks instead of instrumental covers of other peoples' hits, which seems to have been their record company's policy. Last year they covered 'Life Story', one of Jerry Lordan's last tunes. It was the only new thing on a double-CD compilation.

I first started working with Jet when Barry Gibson put together a group called Local Heroes to make a CD, and after that I think we went off to Paris and other places in Europe for appearances. Apart from that, I have only worked with Jet with the Rapiers, Mike Berry and John Leyton, and also with Jet and Pete Oakman, who had his own Bruvvers group after he left Joe Brown. Pete and I used to be with Lonnie Donegan.

Even when Jet was drinking, it was never a problem for me, as I like a drink myself. Since we first started to work together, he has got better and better and continues to do so. Jet gets very nervous before a performance, but that doesn't affect me. He and I often talk about the early days – we were off in different directions. Jet has said, 'Oh, I wish we'd known each other when we were boys.' And I've said, 'It's a good job we didn't meet then!' Thankfully, I *couldn't* handle my drink, so really I couldn't be an alcoholic.

I don't get irritated by Jet or his nerves. We never get that involved where I say, 'For Christ's sake, Jet!' I know he never practises, but if he doesn't work all the time then he should. He's naturally funny and great fun to be with. When he goes on about grockles on the Isle of Wight and anoraks at gigs, he exaggerates. He makes out, 'Oh, bloody anoraks', but he gets inspired by their questions and goes off on stories himself.

Jet's a great survivor and a great musician. Listen to 'Nivram' – a really innovative solo for such a young lad. Listen to *Live At The ABC Kingston* with the swingy little jazz things. Of course, he was into jazz and friendly with all the jazzers before he got into pop. Wherever we are, he always says to me, 'Off we go,' and he finds obscure pubs even though he has been teetotal for years. We've had some good times, both serious and funny, and enjoyed good laughs together. It's a great friendship that we have and he is my best mate.

Janet Harris

JET'S FOURTH WIFE, 1996-2006

I was born in Coronation Road, Aldershot on 27 November 1959. Mother was 39 and dad 63, so I was an afterthought. I have two older brothers: David, born in 1940, and Paul in 1955. David was born to a sailor when mum was young, so his mum was our nana and his sister was mum. It was a lovely childhood in a loving family with lots of presents and even a cup of tea in bed when I was growing up. Mum and dad died when I was still at school. My dad died when I was ten and mum then became an alcoholic.

My brother Paul and I used to watch for my mother from a window. If she walked up the road we were okay and could welcome her home and stay up. If she staggered, we put ourselves to bed to avoid a good hiding. Many a time we had to put her to bed when she passed out. Mother was on Valium, sherry and sleeping tablets, and was sectioned several times. She tried to kill herself six times and succeeded on the seventh attempt. Paul and David are both alcoholics. Paul went through a lot more than I did with our mother. The day she killed herself, I found her and said to him, 'I can't wake mum up.' He said, 'Oh, she's pissed again.' He's suffered all these years with guilt. I was 15½ when she took her life and I'm angry to this day that she left me.

Leaving school I went to work in the Buxted Chicken factory and I loathed alcohol then. I married at 18½, but didn't love him. I just wanted out of the family home, which was left to me and Paul. Paul bought me out. The marriage lasted six months and I started to see another guy, and then found that I was pregnant by him with my daughter, Kim. At this point I left Buxted. We were in love, but split up when Kim was two years old as he wanted to move to the Isle of Wight and I didn't. Ironic really, as that's where we now live. Anyway, when we parted, I bought a mobile home in Farnborough.

When I married my second husband, he took on Kim and we got custody of his son, and then we had a child together in 1985. The marriage lasted until 1989 when we split up. I left him and the children behind and moved to Bournemouth, as my mum always liked it there and it made me feel closer. I worked at BIC – Bournemouth International Centre – as a general assistant and became a senior supervisor, and that's when I met Terry.

As a young girl I'd always liked pop music and singers like Marty Wilde, Billy Fury, Tommy Steele, Adam Faith and Cliff Richard. My elder brother, David, used to bring me their records and I had the pin-up photos on my bedroom walls including Cliff & The Shadows and the Beatles. I wanted to marry Ringo.

We were preparing for a normal concert night at BIC featuring Hank Marvin. The supervisor, who I knew as Galey, and I were discussing catering stock in the afternoon when a man walked through the door. I recognised the face and asked Galey who he was and she knew him straightaway.

I was a very pushy woman and introduced myself and told him that I enjoyed his music. Terry's mate, Brian, asked me if I knew who he was and I told him yes. I asked him if he was staying for the concert and he said he was. Then I asked him if he would still be here on the Tuesday as it was my birthday. Terry said no, but gave me a £5 note out of his wallet and signed it. I still have it. He was a gentleman. I saw him again that evening and he was a little bit pissed. However, we did manage to have a little chat and I didn't get my stocktaking done that night. I realised that there was more to this man than just 'Jet Harris'. He never actually got to see the show as we stayed in the bar talking. The concert finished and Terry was surrounded by fans. I gave my phone number to his friend, Brian, but Terry kept following me and saying, 'Hey, lady!' By this time he was as pissed as a fart.

While in Bournemouth, I lived in a bedsit on my own and started to drink bottles of wine. I went out with my mates, got pissed, and they had to push me home in a shopping trolley. In Bournemouth, I was raped, had an abortion, and didn't want to remember all that stuff.

Terry phoned me two days later and we started seeing each other in Bournemouth and Gloucester, where he lived with his mum. His mum took to me all right. We spent the time doing the pubs and getting wrecked. In January 1996, he moved out of his mum's and I moved in with him in Gloucester, so it was a pretty quick romance. I fell head over heels – we just seemed to connect. Neither of us was looking for a partner and had both given up on the opposite sex. I saw a very vulnerable and kind man, and someone who was going to be kind to me and love me. There was a kind of magic there.

The third floor flat we moved into together was the pits. Terry was unemployed – he didn't even have a guitar – and I'd given up my job. We lived off his dole money, but in the end I got a job in the kitchens of his local pub. Before I did, our days consisted of waiting till pubs opened at 11.00 a.m., having a drink, having a wander around town until he needed a wee, then into another pub for a wee and, of course, another drink. And this was repeated until the pubs closed at 3.00 p.m. I couldn't believe I'd given up my life, such as it was, for this. After a few weeks I'd had enough. I could see my life was going to be one big booze bottle. Then it dawned on me that drink was destroying me. It had destroyed my family and it was destroying Terry, so I stopped drinking.

In 1996, after three or four months living together, Terry went to Italy for 'the treatment'. It was arranged by a man called Barry Gibson, the head of Burns Guitars, who said that we were both going to Italy. Barry was the instigator for getting Terry dry. Somehow we managed to get flight tickets for a journey to Lecco in Italy to visit an Italian psychologist, Amedeo Maffei, who wanted to repay Jet for the pleasure his music had given to him. We were met at the airport by Marco, an interpreter, and on the journey we had to stop so that Terry could get a few beers down to steady himself.

It was really dark when we got there and there were lights outside like torches. Terry and I were absolutely terrified and clung on to each other wondering what we were doing there, in a country we didn't know that had a language we couldn't speak.

We went through an entrance which was similar to a drawbridge. Amedeo and his wife met us and they kept us talking and talking. We'd had nothing to eat and were absolutely shot. Amedeo told us to be up early in the morning as the induction started at 7.00 a.m. We didn't care what time it started, as we weren't gonna do it! The rebels were rebelling.

We were allocated a room in the castle. Amedeo and his family lived in a house in the grounds. It was spooky and you had to press a button for the lights to come on, and then dash to the next floor before they went out.

We went straight to our room without eating. Before we settled down for the night we were given white tracksuits and soled white socks. I had brought a load of clothes, but we had to live in those tracksuits for ten days. Next day, we had breakfast and started the first of many 'induction' courses.

Each 'induction' lasted about an hour and we had three to six per day for the ten days. We went into this room which was fitted out like a recording studio and had four beds. We were wired up so that we could see our heartbeat on screen and also had a pressure band around our foreheads for muscular monitoring. When we put the headphones on, this lovely voice in English made us feel totally relaxed. Our beds were eight feet apart and I felt so relaxed that I fell asleep. At one point the voice told us that we were climbing a mountain in the dark. I hate the dark and was so scared, but mentally I felt Terry hold my hand which was physically impossible because of the eight-foot distance between us.

Amedeo made Terry drink a fusion of artichoke and orange leaves. It made him heave, so I left him to drink it on his own! But he was determined and persevered. During our stay we were well fed, free to explore the premises with its dormitories, showers and rooms, and taken for outings. Amedeo tested Jet's emotions from laughter to tears. Talk of Terry's dad made him cry, as Bill never told Terry that he loved him. In those ten days Terry had no alcohol, no shaking – absolutely dry! While we were exploring in one of the living rooms we came across a cabinet full of booze, but we never touched it. We thought that it

Jet and Janet *(right)* entertain Tony and Sue Meehan
at their home on the Isle of Wight.

was all part of the 'testing'. Amedeo had a large collection of expensive guitars, and he and Terry played together during our stay. It really was a fantastic set-up and Terry was really fortunate to be given the chance to go there. A few years later at a Shadows convention, this American fan came running up to us, 'Jet, you've been there – you've been to the castle! I've told people about it, but nobody believes me!'

After the treatment Jet had two short relapses before he went completely dry. I had to go into hospital for a foot operation and he was upset to be left on his own. He came to see me in hospital pissed as a fart. I was not a happy bunny. When I went home with my foot in plaster to that awful third-floor flat, he was falling on my foot and couldn't understand why I was upset. When he sobered up and realised, he couldn't make it up to me enough: he was so sorry.

The second relapse was on our wedding day, which took place on Monday, 23 December 1996 at Gloucester Registry

Office in Spa Road, Gloucester. I had it all planned beautifully, but he ruined it by getting smashed. Everything was all right when I left the flat in the morning to get my hair done. However, when I got back he was pissed. I was devastated. I kept thinking, *It can't get any worse than this!* That was the last drink he ever had – on 23 December 1996. My last drink was during March of the same year. To make up for the ruined wedding day, on my fortieth birthday he agreed to a wedding blessing with about six close friends in a local church in Upton St Leonards in Gloucester.

Before our marriage, Terry had met up with Laurel Jones, a former friend and musician from the 1970s, and had acquired a guitar. He had to start again and re-learn his hits. After the marriage we lived in accommodation above someone's garage for eighteen months. When we reached the point where we couldn't stand it any longer, we asked the council to help us and they rehoused us in a lovely flat in Cam, which was a poor area.

We kept escaping to the Isle of Wight for holidays. My daughter, Kim, had moved over to the Isle for a holiday and was then expecting a child. By November 1999 we'd had a gutful of living in Gloucester. Our post regularly contained begging letters. People assumed that being 'Jet Harris', we had money. So why were we living in a council house? When we lived in Gloucester, before Terry got dry, we had a budget of £4 a day for his drink and to feed us. We had to avoid the pissheads and went to great lengths to do this, as they were intimidating and wanted money. Everybody thought we had it.

In January 2000 we came to live on the Isle of Wight and have never looked back. It was the best move we have ever made. I've been able to help Terry by organising some aspects of his appearances and seeing to the business side of things. When I first went out to gigs with him, fans used to come up and say things like, 'Jet Harris, I thought you were dead' and 'You used to have hair didn't you?' And to me it was, 'Do you know what he did in 1962?' etc. At first it got to me that people could be so cruel or so thoughtless, but we've heard it all now and it doesn't bother me. When we got together, Terry told me everything about his past that he could remember, so I've never been taken by surprise yet.

Terry and I have helped each other and given each other confidence. Both of us are still developing and moving forward in our lives. We've both been through so much but we are survivors.

Margaret Harris

JET'S THIRD WIFE, 1975-88

When I first met Terry I was 20. I had done sick children's training at home in Scotland and was a qualified nurse. Five of us, including my friend Caroline, went to Jersey to do our RGN and we were all at St Helier Hospital. Caroline and I went for a drink in the Jubilee Hotel in St Helier. He wasn't playing there then, just sitting in the bar I think, and I had no idea who he was. It would be about a month later when he and Paul Wagner started playing as a duet.

It was the night after New Year; we had only been there about a week, and he came over to talk to me when I was sitting with my friend. I was very naïve then. I can't remember what he said, but he asked me to go and speak to him. It was a friendly atmosphere and I felt quite safe. I knew he was a bit drunk, but there again I'd never come across a drinker. As I'm a nice person I was just friendly with him. That was the end of that night, and then I didn't meet up with him until he was walking down the road and I passed him. It wasn't a one-night stand. He was very, very amicable and we started going out. My best friend, Caroline, made up a foursome with his accountant, Malcolm, and eventually married him.

You were drawn to him because you felt sad for him. Terry lived in a B&B near the hospital, so when I went out to town he'd bump into us and we'd walk along the beach with him. He never really spoke about himself then. I still didn't know who he was until a few weeks later when somebody said to me, 'Are you seeing Jet Harris?'

I said, 'No, I've been out with a chap called Terry Harris.'

She said, 'That's him from the Shadows.' Now I'll be honest with you, I'd never heard of Jet Harris or the Shadows. I lived in Scotland, not London. Yes, I knew about Cliff Richard, but I wasn't star-struck.

I don't know if he'd met anybody like me before, because I'm just down to earth, and we became good pals. In fact, if I had known that he was a musician or who he was, I don't think that I would have entertained him. I'm sure I wouldn't have. I would have stopped right there. Certainly at that time I didn't know of his two previous marriages or any children. I think we happened because I got involved with him slowly.

Nine months after we met I moved out of the nursing home and got a flat, as I was classed as 'essentially employed', and we lived together. But it wasn't till we actually stayed together that I started realising he had a problem. His divorce from Susan Speed had come through by this time, and he'd had another girlfriend before me, Anne Fraschetti. When we were together in Jersey he invited her over and she was a really nice person. Anne wouldn't have married him and I don't think she would have even tolerated him. She warned me to get out, as I'd only get hurt.

I met his mum and dad after we'd been together for about a year. They were living in Watford and we went there for the weekend. They were really lovely and both of them were little people. It's sad that his mum was his biggest, biggest crutch. His dad was an introvert, and if you take the drink away from Terry, that's what he was. I think that's what kept me going with him, the introversion. Without the drink he leans on you. I was quiet and shy, but I could stand up for myself and nursing keeps you in touch with the realities of life.

His parents were very kind, but they suffocated him. His mum once told me that to go to school she used to put a hair grip on his hair to keep it back off his eyes. I actually didn't research it, but used to wonder why a nice person like this ended up as an alcoholic. He doesn't deserve it, that's my opinion. His mother didn't want him mixing with 'them black people' who were in London – Terry's mum was a little bit of a snob. To get out of that, he used to drink when he was a young boy because he went around with mummy. He wasn't allowed to mix a lot with other children and the adults around him gave him a taste for drink. To be quite honest, to me, she had him namby-pamby and that's

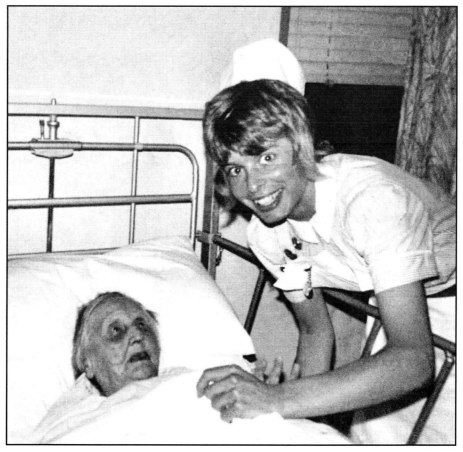

Nurse Harris..

where it began. So, when it got to having to perform anywhere, he couldn't do it without the drink.

Terry's mum wanted him to be *something*, whether it was an athlete or whatever. This was her only child and she never stopped *picking* on him. Terry's dad was gorgeous. He was only about five feet tall and was actually an orphan. He didn't have a lot of personality and was an introvert who didn't have a lot of get up and go. Terry's mum was the driving force, and I believe that most of Terry's introversion came not from his dad's nature, but from his mum's behaviour with Terry.

I think that he did have a wonderful childhood, but in a cocoon, and when he was young he rebelled against his mum and dad. Terry was his mum's pride and joy. She lived for Terry. At the end he had a Jekyll and Hyde relationship with his mother.

His mum had a really good relationship with me. One day she came to see me at work, and we were walking down our ward and I was looking after her. She was a real cockney and she said something to me about Terry and I said, 'Oh, come on, you sound just like Dot Cotton out of *Eastenders* talking about her son, Nick.' But she worshipped the ground that Terry stood on. His mum just stayed in denial over his drinking and behaviour and never questioned his womanising. To her that was just part of him being naughty. She could stand him being an alcoholic, which made him even worse. His mum was an independent little lady and died last year. It was sad, as I had known her since I was 20, but no one told us about his mum's death until after the funeral, and it was a friend who told me.

We lived together for four years in Jersey and he used to binge-drink, and then these binges went into one big, long drink. One night – it's horrible, but I'm going to say it – he battered me, gave me two black eyes and left me in a right state. That must have been about 1972. The only reason was that he wanted to get out to drink and I didn't want him to go, so he went bananas. My friend Caroline insisted I report him to the Centenier, who summoned me into his office. He had the power to remove Terry from the island and asked me if I wanted him to do this, but I didn't want him off of the island.

To cut the story short, he took Terry – under a six-week Section Order – into the psychiatric ward in St Helier Hospital. After five weeks of not seeing him, somebody asked me to go and see him, and he was a different person. He was full of sadness and remorse and wanted to get back.

I had to recover from being emotionally in a turmoil and drained. But then it started getting worse and worse: he continued to batter me and I started letting myself go. He had a power over me. I was a young girl away from my parents. I loved him and I wanted it to work. During our time in Jersey he had lots of little jobs. He did try, give him his due, but it was for drink money.

In 1974 I was down to around six and a half stone and I just couldn't go on. So, I applied to go to Cheltenham to do midwifery and to get away, so that I could concentrate on my career. I had to get away from him: I would've been dead by now. Terry drove to the airport with me. We shook hands and I flew up to Scotland for a visit to family prior to going to Cheltenham. That was the end of the relationship. There was no love lost on my side. If he'd stayed sober, I wouldn't have gone. I'd always felt uncomfortable living with him and never told my parents. They probably did know, but I never told them.

I'd only been there a week, living in the nurses' home, when I got a letter from him. He told me he was living in Cheltenham – which shocked me out of my brain! He'd got himself a flat and a job on the buses, and could I make up with him. He was on the buses for about nine months and did well. Terry had no connections in Cheltenham, he just followed me.

I'd told my parents the relationship was finished and they were pleased for me as they saw this young girl turning into a nervous wreck. Anyway, we made up and I lived with him in Cheltenham. However, when I agreed to go back with him there was a bit of ground-ruling and he was actually sober until we got married. The beatings stopped, but not altogether. My one-year midwifery training ended in March 1975 and we got married on 5 April 1975. After that we moved to Gloucester.

We had our first child, Ben, in 1976. Terry was proud to be a father, but when you needed Terry he wasn't there; he was down in London singing. I wasn't keen on him pursuing a show business career, because to me music equalled alcohol. He couldn't do it without.

Our second son, Sam, was born in 1980, and three months into him being born Terry came home drunk one day. I shouldn't have done it, but I flung the baby chair at him and pushed past him, I was so angry with him for drinking. Ben ran up the stairs, and Terry beat me to a pulp, and I didn't sleep for seven days. Only because he wanted to go back out and drink. It wouldn't have happened if I hadn't flung the chair.

Sometimes there was a funny side, like the time Terry came home aggressively drunk and our dog, Dougal, attacked him by getting hold of his bell-bottom trousers and wrapping them around his legs so that he fell over.

I wouldn't allow that now. I wouldn't even get into a conversation with someone drunk. But then I was a young wife with two little boys whose husband comes home stoned out of his mind. He left me with £2 and went to Jersey for seven days. That's how he used to get rid of his money: as soon as he got a little bit of royalty money, he'd go off on a bender and spend it. Once, Terry had gone from Gloucester to Portsmouth to see another musician and it cost me £159 as, having no money, he returned from Portsmouth in a taxi! It's not just the alcoholic who suffers; the family suffers as well. All of us, including the dogs and cats, should have been on Valium.

After that beating, I didn't get the police in and my friend down the road saw me all right. It's so sad, but I wouldn't do it now. When I think of my stupidness I get very angry. To let somebody do that to you! It was then that I went to the organisation Alanon, which is for the families of alcoholics. They tell you that if somebody wants to drink, then let them. From then on, I let Terry do what he wanted. If he wanted to drink, I never stopped him, and he never hit me again. It only happened when I tried to stop him from drinking. I should have left him.

We had bought a house by then using both of our monies. He had the deposit as a result of a royalty cheque when the Shadows had a No.1 album of their greatest hits and I was in regular work. In fact, both with Ben and Sam, I never stopped working. I sound as if I'm a right martyr, but that's how it was. I did night duty, so the children either stayed at home, or somebody would look after them. He looked after them – he loved his children. It wasn't all bad.

The longest period of soberness Terry had in our marriage was about two years. That was a good time, and I'll tell you when that was: it was when he took up photography and he did not play music. He gave up photography because people pushed him back to play. In actual fact, if he'd stayed with the photography, he may well have stayed sober. He couldn't go on stage without drink or drugs because he's introverted. When he was doing the photography in Gloucester, we lived down this

Family man Jet with Ben and Maggie.

little lane and I think that's the happiest that we were. If you can say anything about Terry and I, it's that we were good pals.

In 1985 I was six months pregnant with Craig, who was born on 10 January 1986, and Terry was still sober, when he wanted to go back on the road. Eight months into the pregnancy and Terry started getting a bit erratic. In, out, in, out – can't stay in the house. He'd started show business again and he was drinking again. One day I said to him, 'I want you to stand there and tell me exactly what's wrong with you. Is it drink? Have you got a brain tumour?' He told me that he was in love with this other woman who he'd met some years before when he was drying out in some psychiatric hospital.

After I had got over the initial shock, over the period of a week, I said to him as a friend, 'If you're in love with somebody, you'll stay in a tent, so move out.' He said, 'Just let me see her when I want – for sex.' I told him that was not on. I'm not being big-headed, but the only reason he went with her was because I was pregnant and he doesn't like bumps near him in the bed. And when I needed him, he shit on me. Terry was my world and the dad of the boys, and we were about to have another little boy. I was hurt, but I was prepared to let him see her as long as he told me the truth. I told him that if he told me any more lies, he was out. He told me a lie that he hadn't seen her on a particular day and he had, and that was it.

However, he didn't leave us and stay away. Between 1986 and 1987 he used to come backward and forward. When Craig was about ten days old he stayed over. He got up about six in the morning and had three bottles of wine, four miniature whiskies and four cans of beer. And that was before the doctor came to see me for my post-natal at nine o'clock! That's the truth. I don't know how he's still alive, but somebody looks after us all and he's alive for a reason.

Terry stayed with the other woman for about a year, and she was his manager. When their relationship ended, he came back to us and I let him stay in a caravan in the garden. We got divorced in 1988 when Craig was going on for three, and he's just turned 19.

There was a man in my life after Terry moved out and Craig was born. Being vulnerable, when someone shows you a little bit of love and buys you flowers, you jump into bed with them – which is what happened to me – but it was a mistake and the relationship didn't last long.

The sad thing is that Terry has never paid maintenance. He got a court order to pay the children 'x' amount a month and we got divorced just before the CSA came in. My parents used to get livid at me, but I've never really pushed it. The thing is, that it was his choice. As they said at the Alanon meetings, 'Live and let live'. He has to live with the fact that he never brought his children up or paid for his children. Mind, he used to give me the odd £100, but that was in recent years.

Other women have organised and managed him, but with me I had my job and he was standing on his own two feet. He wasn't the weaker partner with me. It wasn't really the alcohol – I would have put up with that. If it hadn't been that he'd stuck his penis in an affair, I would still be with that man. To be quite honest, he wasn't a stud or a lover. Terry's a man who just wants to get on with the job, which probably goes back to his groupie days. When I asked him what was the difference between the other woman and me sex-wise, he said to me, 'Well, you're the wife' – meaning that I was available. I said, 'Well, now you've got two *skivvies*, she can wash your *skiddies*!' He didn't think that was very funny.

I've met Billie Davis several times, and she's a really nice person who wouldn't stand any nonsense. Terry was very bitter over Carol Costa, but didn't go on about her or that period of his life. Sadly, some women have just used him and behaved like groupies. Terry comes across as a great womaniser, but to be quite honest he wasn't. I would think that, in Terry's life, every woman has gone with him because he's been in a pub.

If he was going through his star years now like today's pop people and celebrities, the media would have a field day with him. If his health could survive it, he would do well on one of those *I'm A Celebrity... Get Me Out Of Here!* shows, and he'd be good fun. The other thing that's good about him is that he can put his hand to anything. He's articulate and very clever. He's also a very sensitive person and a perfectionist. Terry is obsessional, and if you ask him to do something he'll spend hours getting it perfected.

His other plus points are his little personality and his humour. He's good fun and has got a brilliant, dry sense of humour, and we batted off one another. Apart from the humour, I'm probably the exact opposite. I'm not into the *twang-twang* music, and the thing that used to annoy him about me is that I said to him once – probably more than once – that all those instrumentals he played with the Shadows sound the same to me.

He phoned me up one day just before I knew he'd gone off with Janet, and he was begging to come back because he was living with his mother. He said to me, 'Are you ever fucking going to have me back!?' And I said, 'Terry, I'm on night duty.' He'd woke me up. I got a 'f— this' and a 'f— that'.

The next thing I knew was that he'd got married, and that

was only about two months later! He always marries the people for security, because he's never, ever grown up and been independent. Janet is a lovely person and he'll never come here as long as Janet keeps him there. I think with Terry's marriages he's a bit like the Richard Burton and Elizabeth Taylor types – these people, instead of just living with each other, have to get married. You know: get married, get married, get married.

The thing that I'll always, always be grateful to Terry for was that he gave me three lovely sons, and the oldest one reminds me of Terry. I'm not saying that we didn't have good times; we *did* have good times. I would've put up with any amount of drink that Terry drank because I knew that alcoholism is an illness.

During our marriage, he wasn't an alcoholic every day. An alcoholic is always an alcoholic, but Terry was a binge-drinker. He'd go weeks without drinking. Sometimes, I think his true partner has been a bottle. Take the drink away and Terry would've been all right. My friend said that we'd always get back together, but it would be in different circumstances, because since Terry left me I've grown up a lot. I grew up with him and we had some great fun. I have some beautiful photos of him and the boys.

It was hard on the boys when they were younger. Other kids at school used to say to them, 'If your dad's Jet Harris, why haven't you got a big house?', 'I've seen your dad delivering papers', etc. Kids like to impress their friends.

I went to work one night – we were married at the time – and the front page news of the *News of the World* was JET HARRIS'S WIFE SLEEPS WITH CLIFF RICHARD. Not his *ex*-wife – *wife*! Colleagues asked me, 'Have you slept with Cliff Richard!?'

Later, Jet got £10,000 for saying that he slept with Cliff's sister, Donna. It couldn't have been true – she wouldn't have had him. People told me that a lady known to Jet had gone to the papers and told them, 'Terry's gone off with Donna.' At the time Donna was down in Gloucester, and a friend, a nice person.

It didn't make the front page, but something like page 7, and that lady probably got money from that newspaper. They have to get a reply, so they asked Terry and he got £10,000 from them. He said that Donna was the love of his life – he had to make it worth the £10,000 he got for it. And his boys had to go to school with this business.

That was bloody hurtful that one. Kids would tell them, 'Oh, your dad never loved your mum.' They didn't deserve that, and they never saw any of the money. I asked him why he had said that about Donna to the papers, and he said, 'Well, they were going to pay me, so I had to say something.' I don't think he actually said that they had sex and slept together.

Janet does everything for him and puts a cocoon around him. She's twenty years younger than him and was a great fan of Terry's from his Shadows days. He's not the kind of man who would meet you and make a play for you, and he's not romantic or a sex symbol. He might have been one in his Shadows days. I think he's definitely got charisma. It's so sad.

I could write a book about all the hangers-on in his life that he has paid. He's always got to have a man friend. When we were in Jersey, he bought this chap this and that. It's weird, because other people like his family couldn't get a penny out of him.

I don't know, but I wouldn't have thought that he's given up drink. You know what happens? You'll go for a coffee in a pub and then he'll go to the toilet, nips to the bar for a whisky, and then comes back to his coffee. I hope to God that he has been cured. Over the years a lot of people have been disgusted with him, but he has brought it on himself and he's gone down that path himself. If it wasn't for Janet looking after him, I don't know where he would be, I'm sure. I think he now suffers from chronic selfishness. Probably he is the love of my life, but I think he has gone through life thinking everyone thinks the best of him. Sadly, Terry has never sat down and thought, *Gosh! What have I done?*

Wee Willie Harris

PERFORMER

Jet worked with me in 1957 and 1958 for six or seven months when he was the bass player with Tony Crombie & His Rockets, who backed me on stage shows.

Tony Crombie was a jazzman and wouldn't stand for any nonsense. If one of his band played out of tune, I would hear Tony scream, 'Get off, tune up, and come back on!' The musician wouldn't be missed for a few minutes as the band had a bass player, two guitars, drums, two tenor saxes and a baritone. The idea was for me to front a driving band playing riffs while I belted it out like Little Richard.

My pink hair gimmick was down to Paul Lincoln who co-owned the 2I's coffee bar and also Lincoln Promotions with his partner, Ray Hunter. Paul and Ray were wrestlers who came over from Australia, bought the 2I's and set up as rivals to Dale Martin Wrestling Promotions, who controlled British Wrestling. I was the first with the coloured hair gimmick. One day, when we were playing Leeds, we were in Bob Barclay's club. Bob was a trombone player, and I had gone for something to eat in his back room when in comes Jimmy Savile, who was a Leeds dancehall deejay. He asked me what it was like to go around with pink hair. I didn't know it, but he was picking my brain, and when I saw him next he had one half of his head white and the other half black!

I got on well with Jet and had no problems, and somewhere I have a photo of me onstage with Jet behind. Jet had bad nerves before a show. We all have nerves before we go on, but he used to pace up and down and I'd say, 'For Gawd's sakes, stand still, you'll get me at it!' For some reason he was extremely nervous. Perhaps it was a lack of confidence. He wasn't drinking then – Tony Crombie wouldn't have stood for it.

Jet was one of the first bass players to switch from

Wee Willie in action, 1959.

stand-up bass to bass guitar, and I think he sent to the States to get it. I don't think Jet must have got on with Tony, as Tony gave him the tin-tack*. On tour, Jet went with me to see my aunty in Yorkshire and enjoyed hotpot for the first time.

Lennie Hastings, a big blond fellow, took over from Jet with the stand-up bass and we had to place a mike near him to amplify the sound. Ronnie Verrel, the drummer with Ted Heath, used two foot pedals to make the bass sound. Ted Heath was also one of the first to have his drums lit up, which many of the pop acts did later on. Some of the jazz boys wouldn't play rock'n'roll; they said they'd rather starve. They forgot that Little

---

* Sack.

Richard and Bill Haley had very competent musicians in their bands.

After Tony Crombie, I worked with many artists and was on bills with Cliff & The Shadows. I even sang for Cliff one night when his voice was bad. I went on and stood – in clear view of the audience – at the back with the drummer and did three or four of his numbers, starting with 'Move It', while Cliff was up front doing his leg movements and curling his lip. No one in the audience realised. Funnily enough, Brian Bennett, who later replaced Tony Meehan in the Shadows, used to be my washboard player.

Frank Ifield

PERFORMER

There is no denying the fact that the Shadows were, and still are, the most professional instrumental group it has been my pleasure to work with. Even in their early days, it was easy to spot their unique potential.

Whenever the curtains would open on their act, the audience reaction could be heard a mile away. Yet the feminine squeals of delight were not for the incredibly talented lead guitarist Hank B. Marvin, nor were they swooning over the best rhythm guitarist in the business, Bruce Welch. Even their drummer Tony Meehan, who would have ranked as among the finest in Britain even by today's standards, was not the focus of their attention being hidden behind his kit. No! The screams, usually reserved for their former lead singer and superstar Cliff Richard, were now being directed at this young, fair-haired Adonis who played the bass guitar. His name was Jet Harris, and I couldn't help thinking that the raging hormones of the teenage girls in the audience were giving voice to their choice of Jet as a promising new star in the making.

With such overt adulation, I suppose it was only inevitable that Jet should begin to set his sights on breaking away to go solo. I recall thinking the kid's got guts to relinquish the comfort and security of being a founding member of such a highly creative and successful band. It certainly wouldn't be easy for a bassman to become a star in his own right, so when he and Tony Meehan teamed up and their first single, 'Diamonds', was a big hit, I could only admire him for his dogged conviction. Certainly, the successful record sales they enjoyed could be taken as absolute proof of his dedicated following.

My first meeting with Jet was when the Shadows first joined our management agency in Savile Row with my Australian manager, Peter Gormley. I remember that Jet was quoted in an article in the *New Musical Express* as saying that his initial impression of me was that I appeared like a Hollywood cowboy who seemed out of place in the city. My first impression of Jet was that he was shy and retiring.

The last time I saw him was in the 1990s at a mutual friend's house. The signs of the passing years were written on both of our smiles, yet despite the many stories he told me of his wilful life, I still recognised that same quiet, self-effacing side of him coming through.

Jet will always hold a position in my mind as a man who was never afraid to forge his own way and, with great impetuosity, stare destiny in the face – and laugh.

Laurel Jones

MUSICIAN

It was 1973 or 1974 when Jet knocked on my door in Cheltenham. He was on the buses then and I was working in local boozers playing Shadows music. They were hard days for my wife and I, who had to take bottles back for the deposits. Someone brought an acoustic guitar for Jet to play and I ended up strumming. He asked me if I wanted to form a band, but nothing came of it. I lost track of him, then I moved to a new house in Sun Street, Cheltenham and he came to my door with drummer Ken Newman and rhythm guitarist Jimmy Sloane.

Being an alcoholic, I was doing a lot of shaking at the time. Jet was drinking and trying to play lead, but it wasn't working – they wanted me to play lead, so that Jet could go back to bass. They took me to the Red Lion pub which was managed by Jimmy Budd, but I told them that I couldn't play or hold the guitar properly. Jet got a few beers into me to steady me up and I was okay.

Roger LaVern, the keyboard player with the Tornados, managed the group. We had Epiphones then, but the sound was hopeless. One day Terry left me a tenner to get some flagons, and when he came back he gave me a Fender Strat. God knows where he got it from – it must've been the *Exchange & Mart*.

I was green in those days! I recall we played at Covent Garden's Rock Garden. Me and Jet got in the club first and there was only the barman there. He warned us that there was to be no 'smoking' in there that night, and I asked, 'Haven't you any ashtrays?' In disbelief, Jet turned to me and said, 'You *twat!*'

After Roger LaVern quit, Jimmy Budd financed the group and became our manager. I wanted us to sound like a '60s band, so I suggested we call ourselves 'The Diamonds', after Jet's hit. Jimmy Sloane went and Graham Sayce replaced him, so there was

Jet with friend Laurel Jones in 1997.

him, me, Kenny and Jet.

Jet and I were always shaking and skint then because of the drink, whereas the others had all their money. We were in Scotland and Graham Sayce said, 'What would you like a *half* of?' I won't tell you what we said!

We had a gypsy caravan, but playing seaside places they wouldn't let us park up. We played Wooky Hollow Club in

138

Liverpool and they had a good comedian, Joe, who introduced the acts and had his own turn there every week. He spotted our gypsy caravan and said to the punters, 'Jet Harris and his gang of gypsies are here this week – better watch your pockets!' Joe was always saying we were selling clothes pegs and heather. So, at the end of the week we got our own back: we bought a load of those long, wooden clothes pegs and showered the stage from the audience when he said it on stage.

At Rivelin Dams, Sheffield – the Shadows used to go there, it was all clear water and hills – we decided to dry out for a couple of days and go walking with the rest of the band. It was steeper than we thought and, when I was halfway up, I found I had left my tobacco tin on a rock. I asked Terry if he could get it for me and he said, 'I can't bloody move, Laurel!' The height had made him freeze. At the end of that, Terry had to walk two miles round to get back to where we'd started. When we got back, we ended up having a couple of pints in a pub – some drying-out day!

Another time we had a week in Maesteg, Wales. We arrived on Sunday to do Monday-to-Saturday and had our little caravan with us. Now, Terry was a quick thinker drinkwise. We couldn't get a drink, so me and Graham Sayce went up this hill. In them days Terry wore a black mac, and we hadn't seen him for a good hour. We looked down and saw this black figure like Batman flying down the street. It was a market day and he'd found an open pub! I could've killed him, as I was stuck up the hill with Graham the half-pint man! Terry was good at finding pubs and has a nose for it.

I used to drink Strongbow cider and, going to Belfast, had three full crates as a seat in the van as a back-up, as I didn't think we could buy them there. We had to be drunk in those days to play. Terry and I used to think it was great if we could get an apple down our throats as food.

About seven years ago we were with P.J. Proby for a barbecue in the back garden of his London home. Alan Lovell of the Swinging Blue Jeans was there, and Beaky from Dave Dee's group. The only ones not drinking were the three alcoholics. Jim Proby had a great stock of booze and said he was saving it for a big occasion.

I've been dry for fourteen years – it doesn't even bother me now. I'm playing in a local band and doing a cleaning job. If Terry needs me, I'm there. But if he kicks off a new band and I'm in it, then, when we're established, I get pushed into the shadows – no pun intended – by the London boys.

It was my doctor who put me off drink. He told me that the next stop was the graveyard and that got through. I'm on Hemineverin. I take two at night and I fall asleep quickly. On the advice of my mate, Terry, I took the Hemineverin and drank – but it didn't work! Keith Moon took thirty in a hit and didn't drink anymore, did he? I understand that George Best had them sewn into his stomach.

The last time Terry 'found' me was in the early '90s when he had left Jackie and he came to see me with a gypsy pal. He was in a right state, but had driven over, and his pal stank to high heaven. I gave them a few cans in the kitchen. My wife had just done the washing and the gypsy sat on it. It went back in the washer when he left!

That night, he took me back to Gloucester with them to a gig where an Irish band were performing at a caravan club. Terry was going to do a turn there, but when he got onstage he couldn't play. He looked over at me with those big, sad eyes, so I got up and did 'Ghost Riders In The Sky' and that satisfied them.

Afterwards we were all too drunk to drive, but I didn't want to be stuck in a dosshouse with those two all night. I drove five miles an hour down three roads – or that's what my eyes saw. When I thought about the carnage I could have caused, I never drove again, even when I got dry.

John Leyton

PERFORMER

I can't really give you dates, but the first time I recall meeting Jet was on a tour that I did in the '60s. It was a Robert Stigwood promotion and I topped it. Mike Sarne was in it, Mike Berry, Billie Davis and Jet Harris & Tony Meehan.

The very last tour I did in that sort of chapter of my life was in February 1964. That was with the Rolling Stones and I don't know whether Jet was on that, or my earlier tour in 1963. Certainly Jet was going out with Billie.

Personally, I thought – and this is no disrespect to the other Shadows, as they were and are a very fine band of musicians with a lot of charisma – that Jet stood out in terms of charisma. He was a good-looking lad, and I know that the fans liked him and he must have got the bulk of fan letters for the Shadows. The name too is a great name: Jet Harris. And he did stand out with his blond hair.

Obviously, even though we were travelling separately most of the time, you get to know most people. In those days, I didn't really get to know him. I don't think anybody did on the tour really. I'm not saying he was unfriendly, but he wasn't forthcoming in any way. I suppose in a way a bit of a loner who kept himself to himself, and I suppose could be, at times, I can imagine, depending on how much he'd been boozing, a bit on the argumentative side. I never, ever saw him the worse for drink onstage – ever. It was a bit like the actor Trevor Howard, really: he was a drinker, but I never saw him the worse for it in front of the camera or onstage. No, Jet was always, as far as I can remember, totally professional in that respect.

However, I do remember one incident on this tour. I can't really remember where we were going – presumably we were coming from London – but we stopped off at one of those road cafés they had at that time. Whether we arranged to do it or it was purely coincidental I have no idea. Mike Sarne was there, Jet was there, Billie Davis was there and I was there. I can't remember anybody else. I don't really know what transpired in the café. All I know is that Mike Sarne left the café and gave Billie Davis a lift in his car. I remember the car because it was a Thunderbird with the soft top and it was a nice day and they had the hood down. I remember him leaving with Billie Davis in the passenger seat. Whether she'd pitched up at the café with Mike Sarne or pitched up at the café with Jet I've no idea. But all I do know is that three or four minutes after they had left, Jet appeared in an absolute rage, a furious mood. He, at the time, I believe, was driving a Volvo like the one the Saint used to drive in that series, and he had discovered that Billie Davis had gone off with Mike Sarne.

Anyway, I left to go on to wherever we were going and had left Jet at the café in a total rage. I don't know whether an argument had taken place, or what had happened. So I'm driving along and all of sudden, after about three or four minutes, this Volvo with Jet behind the wheel comes up from behind and overtakes me on a blind bend. I imagine he was approaching 100 miles an hour. It was quite frightening the way he was driving it: he was very, very lucky not to have had a serious accident and at the same time take somebody with him. He was overtaking cars in front of me, going like a bat out of hell round blind bends. It was unbelievable, and what he was doing, he was trying to catch up Mike Sarne and Billie Davis. What it was all about I've no idea. That's just an incident I remember.

I had no problems with Jet. As I say, he and Tony were on my show. Perhaps if I had been on their show things may have been a bit more difficult.

After that, you'd have to fast forward to the present day really, for the next time I saw him was when I appeared with him in the Isle of Wight a few years ago. I was shocked, because he is virtually unrecognisable from how he used to look. Yet, onstage today he's got a wonderful dry sense of humour, which I suppose he always has had, but somehow that sense of humour seems to suit him better as an older man, than it did when he was young.

When I was first invited on to the show, I thought, *Well, Jet doesn't sing. How on earth is he going to hold an audience playing bass guitar?* But I must say I was very impressed with how he puts his act together and his dry sense of humour. He is exceptionally laid-back, which is absolutely perfect. And today I admire him enormously for having given up the drink, because it would have killed him, and I believe it nearly did. I don't think people who have been alcoholics can go back and drink in moderation, and I think Jet realises that.

Gene Vincent, who also drank heavily, pulled a gun out on me. He was barmy. I remember I was backstage with him – maybe Jet was in that show, but I can't remember him – Billy Fury was in the dressing room as well, when Gene pulled a bloody pistol out of his pocket. Whether it was loaded or not, I've no idea, but he waved it around at all of us and told us to back off. Oh dear – *dreadful!*

Brian 'Licorice' Locking

MUSICIAN

We had a skiffle group in Grantham, Lincolnshire, my hometown, called the Vagabonds. There was Roy Taylor – who is now Vince Eager – on vocals and guitar, Mick Fretwell on drums, Roy Clark played rhythm guitar, and I was on double bass. I recall I first met Jet when we went to see a show at Nottingham in 1957 with Wee Willie Harris and he was playing with a group called the Most Brothers and in Tony Crombie's band.

After the show we went backstage and met Jet and some of the others. Later, we got in a van and went back to Grantham, where we went to Roy Taylor's house. We had a bit of a party really – not a wild party, just tea, cakes and whatever – which they appreciated.

After that, our group, the Vagabonds, entered into a skiffle competition and we got to the area final, which we won. This meant that we were on a *Come Dancing* national competition in London at the Locarno in Streatham. We went there and came second, won £100. It was then that we went to the 2I's coffee bar and we played down there before going back home. After that, we got a call from Paul Lincoln of the 2I's asking if we would like to play there regularly, which we did. We left home, the four of us, and that's where we met up with Jet and Wee Willie again on odd occasions when they wandered in.

Jet's hair was reasonably blondish then and he was playing with Tony Crombie's Rockets. I thought he was a nice guy and a nice player. I didn't see a lot of him, he was more like a casual acquaintance really. I remember – I think it was in Wardour Street – I went down there and there was a guy there called Pepe Rush who used to make amplifiers. I think it was there where I met Jet, who had a double bass then. I think it was a full-size Hawkes concert model. Just on odd little occasions we met. At that time I had no inkling about any drinking. He just seemed to be an accomplished player who was well popular.

It sort of developed, our little band, and we went on tour as the Vagabonds with Wee Willie. Jet was also on the tour with Tony Crombie's Rockets. He was his own person, a bit on the quiet side, but I wouldn't say he was morose. He just got on with the job. His time with the Vipers was just before we went down there. Our group was very much influenced by the Vipers in actual fact, but I think they'd gone by the time we went to the 2I's.

In 1958 I was doing a tour with Terry Dene and we were at the Alhambra Theatre, Bradford, when I went into a café and this record came on called 'Move It'. It was brilliant, this Cliff Richard guy. We heard a short time after that the Drifters, Cliff Richard's backing group, consisted of Jet, Tony, Bruce and Hank. We could have been a part of that originally, but after Terry Dene we were touring with Vince Taylor and Marty, so we were off the scene. They went down to the 2I's to see what personnel were available. It could have been Tony Sheridan, but it was Hank and Bruce who were recommended, with Jet and Tony, who was a genius of drummer – and only 15, coming on board later after Terry Smart and Ian Samwell departed. A lot of water had gone under the bridge by the time Jet joined the Drifters.

After that, I saw him working on an *Oh Boy!* show when I was with Vince Taylor. So, there wasn't a lot of contact at all. I remember once going to a party and Jet was there. He probably had some problem and there was just the hint that he'd been drinking. He lost his rag over something and didn't stay. I didn't bother to enquire, but there was the general feeling that he had problems.

I was gobsmacked when I was asked to replace him in the Shadows. I thought my career was over. I'd come to the end of the line and I didn't know where to go next. Everything had just finished. And I suddenly get a call from Brian Bennett – right out of the blue, mind you – telling me that Jet was going to leave, or had left, and would I be ready for an audition. So, I went to Brian's house for a rehearsal/audition and got the part. I'd worked with Brian before and he'd left to join the Shadows when

145

we were both on tour with Tommy Steele. So, we were back together; we were a bit of a team really.

To be honest – and this is absolutely true – I was always aware that Jet is a hard act to follow. We couldn't have been more different, could we? Totally different. I was always conscious that it was a bit of a tough task – because of his image, and I wasn't the blond, moody type. And he was so popular it was ridiculous. He was the kingpin for looks. I was a completely different kettle of fish. I've always respected him and even now he comes out with some great performances – by virtue of what he plays: 'Applejack', 'Diamonds', and all that kind of thing. He's very, very competent indeed. Jet's been improving all the time – beyond measure. I knew he was a jazzer, and there's a lot of hidden talent there that's never come out yet.

I remember seeing a bass guitar for the first time down the 2I's being played in a resident group called the Worried Men, who were Adam Faith's backing group. Anyway, I remember them playing a Framus bass guitar which they'd brought down. I remember seeing Jet having a tootle on it. I can't recall the bass player's name, just that his voice was very, very, husky. I wouldn't touch it – it was a new thing. I was a double bass player and I was *frightened* of the blooming thing!

I hadn't seen him for about twenty-odd years and it's only about eight years ago that we met up. He was doing something with the Local Heroes and Barry Gibson. They were doing a show in Paris and Jet was on the bill, and I was asked to go along. Bruce, Cliff Hall, Clem Cattini, Alan Jones – it was, like, a Shadows thing and a good package. We've been in touch on and off since. We often meet at *Shadowmania*, or odd gigs we might meet up with Jet and Janet. End of story. Jet's done absolutely magnificently in giving up alcohol. If I had a hat I would take it off to him.

Tony Meehan

MUSICIAN

The truth is very cruel. Jet Harris was the one in one million who blew it. He wanted to waste his life away and he did. Jet was a very, very brilliant musician who went to pieces. I couldn't venture to guess why, but his first wife was a very hard character who I did not like, and she had her eyes set on Cliff.

I was probably the first to come across her affair with Cliff Richard and all of us told Cliff to pack it in and leave them alone. Carol's affair with Cliff only lasted about six months. To my knowledge, Cliff was never interested in girls and I think that Carol was his first and only serious affair. Why did she do it? She was a woman, and who knows what women want? Women want power.

Cliff and Jet were rivals, and in a strange way there was an attraction between them. In cases like that sometimes the woman is 'taken out'. Cliff really didn't love Carol. Jet always liked a drink, but the drinking accelerated over Carol. Whatever the reasons, Jet had major problems.

When I joined the group I was a 15-year-old boy, and not a man. We toured constantly, doing shows twice nightly and three times on Saturdays, and never got a holiday and rarely a day off. My timekeeping problem was probably due to physiological reasons caused by constant tiredness, but I did what I had to do as far as the music was concerned. Initially, we had a unique quality. We were all from different backgrounds, but the chemistry was there and very good. We could be very volatile, but we were creating something and trying to find ourselves.

With the Shadows I toured the US, South Africa and Scandinavia. When we did a six-month season at the Palladium, they had to start without me as I was taken ill. It doesn't often get recognised, but we changed world music. There wouldn't have

Tony visits Jet, 2004.

been any Beatles, Rolling Stones or Gerry & The Pacemakers if it hadn't have been for us.

Bruce Welch had a difficult manner – to do with his upbringing I suppose. When I joined the Drifters, Jet was the best musician and the group leader. Bruce wanted to be leader, but being the worst musician of the group he couldn't get the respect. Not long before he died, Peter Gormley told me that Bruce Welch *destroyed* the Shadows: he took over and was domineering.

After approximately eighteen months, I left the Shadows around November 1961, at the end of our season in Blackpool, and went to work at Decca Records as a session musician, producer and arranger. There were no regrets; I did what I wanted to do.

I was living in America in the 1970s when I heard that Bruce and Olivia Newton-John had broken up. I went to see him, stayed with him and comforted him.

At Decca, I played on Jet's recordings of 'Besame Mucho', 'Man With The Golden Arm' and 'Some People'. It was Jerry Lordan who came up with 'Diamonds' and suggested that it would be perfect for a six-string bass and drums.

It took two or three days to record 'Diamonds'. Jet was ill and had difficulty learning it. When we got around to recording 'Scarlett O'Hara' and 'Applejack', Jet was very sick by that time, couldn't learn the numbers and was nowhere to be found. Sometimes he would turn up and sometimes he didn't. You didn't know how you would find him and my nerves were ragged. A session musician, Joe Moretti, played on those records, but Decca put Jet's name on it to sell them.

He was so destructive in every way – look at the lives of people he has affected. Jet and I could have had the most fantastic career together, but he blew it.

With Jet Harris you're talking about one of the most famous musicians in the world. He was a very creative man and I believe that we would still have been going today. When our duo broke up I was upset, as we both had a strong affection for what we were doing. We had been booked on a tour and I finished the contract with the Tony Meehan Combo.

Jet once told me that he kept a half-bottle of vodka by his

bed. When he woke up in the morning, he drank half of the half-bottle. Then he put some Worcestershire sauce on his tongue to get his juices going before having some sweet tea. This was followed by the remaining vodka and then he went down to the pub. He would drink two bottles of vodka and ten pints of beer a day, and that was his life for years. I talked to the Italian psychologist who cured him, and he told me that it was all to do with Jet's father, but that he will never drink again.

We won't be getting together again, either as Jet & Tony or the Shadows. It's forty years too late.

Alec Merrick

FRIEND AND ROADIE

Jet and I worked at Marian Electronics in Chalford, Gloucestershire, where we built fruit machines and, as we had the same sense of humour and interest in music, we hit it off straightaway. I had been a military drummer and then went into groups. Starting time at Marian was 8.00 a.m. – early if you're on the booze. When he came in to start work, I would say, 'Good morning, Ter,' and he would say, 'What's fucking good about it, having to come into this fucking place?' If I remember correctly, Jet was registered disabled because of his liver and had been in the Coney Hill Nursing Home. Jet went for his interview in his suit and tie, and called the boss 'Sir'. They assessed me for employment – I was chosen to be an electrician because of my manual dexterity as a musician.

At our ten-minute tea break, it was up to the Red Lion pub in Chalford for a pint of lager and double gin-and-orange – in ten minutes! It was sixty seconds' drive each way, which left us eight minutes for drinking. Ray Brown, the Red Lion's landlord, who had a large wife called Bette who used to put her corsets on the radiator to dry off, used to go with a fellow landlord, Ivor Dugdale, and get rat-arsed at another pub.

At Marian Electronics we were all at drinking. One guy, Dougie Pickles, used to hide in the corner and get rat-arsed. When they made him a supervisor, he changed completely! The factory was on a millpond and the pond was full of bottles. Jet worked with his back to an open window, so getting rid of the empty bottles was easy. Usually, buying the liquor and drinking it is the easy part – getting rid of the fucking empties is the problem. I knew one bloke in Gloucester whose wife plagued him to dig the garden, but he couldn't because of all the bottles he'd buried in it!

After Marian Electronics moved to Briscombe, Jet found a Spar shop nearby that would sell him drink in the mornings and in the ten-minute morning break. In place of the eight-minute session in the Red Lion, he'd take a half-bottle of vodka and sit in the hills above the factory contemplating how to give up drinking!

When he was living with his mother, Wyn, and still at Marian Electronics, we had a gig in three days' time and when we were driving past a pub called the Walnut Tree, I wouldn't let him have one. Further down the road, I heard him giggling. He had a six-pack in the back! 'I knew you wouldn't stop,' he said.

In the '80s, Jet had cut down on the drink and the promoter Hal Carter was doing a CD for Jet. He got it going and, as a result, Jet was offered a place on an *Oh Boy!* tour with Eden Kane, the Vernons Girls, the Dallas Boys, Jet and the Diamonds (actually the Tornados), Mike Berry & The Outlaws, Billie Davis, John Walker and a wonderful guy called Leighton Summers, who did Elvis Presley songs.

Jet always said that one day we would go on the road together, and one day he turned up in his red Capri and said, 'I'm ready – do you want to drive?' He never forgot. The tour was for three to four months, and, as Jet couldn't drive because he was banned, he asked me to be his road manager, and I did this for over two years. I knew it would be hard work and a full-time job looking after Jet Harris, as he was on a relapse. I stayed with him and got him the halves of bitter – as long as Hal Carter didn't find out – 'cause I understood his need. Hal gave me strict instructions to control Jet's drinking. I met Hal Carter for the first time at the Lakeside, Camberley. Jet and I had had a drink at the Wheatsheaf pub nearby. As soon as he saw me, he grabbed me and asked if Jet had been drinking. I told him no, and he said, 'If he does, tell me and I'll tell people he's ill and he won't go on.'

When he was living in Reservoir Road, Gloucester, with his manager, Jackie, I'd been with him all night at a gig with Chris Black & Black Cat and the Tornados. Jet was performing on his own then and he took ill between sets. He had ulcers inside and outside his mouth. He was still up and about, but his body was telling him enough was enough. I just stayed with him to make sure that he was all right, but he was unaware of the state he was in.

Once at Dingwall's Club in London's Camden Lock, I had to physically restrain him. You could see the dressing room door backstage from the audience and Mike Franklin, Jet's guitarist in the Strangers, opened the door and the audience caught Jet standing there with no trousers. Jet was very embarrassed and angry, and was going to go for Mike, but I calmed the situation down.

Jet was terribly on edge before going onstage, and I tried to calm him down and get him crafty halves of beer. On the tours everybody mucked in together. The Dallas Boys and the Vernons had played all the pits, so you had to become one of the pack – they wouldn't let you be otherwise. We had a routine to make sure we had everything and there wasn't a lot of bother. Our cars were mainly old bangers doing 35 miles per hour. The cops stopped us for going so slow on the motorway, but they didn't notice that we'd both had a drink! Travelling is a hard life – people don't realise. The public buy their ticket and they want you to entertain them.

Hal Carter was a real character and you had no trouble getting money from him. At Heathrow Airport once, he came swanning through wearing a smart suit and his fedora. The Dallas Boys broke into 'Pretty Flamingo' and Hal played it up. On another occasion, Hal was asked to deliver a warning message to Jet from one of the other artists he represented, Billy Fury. Jet had let it be known that he fancied Billy's girl, Fran, and Fury asked Hal, 'Tell Harris that the stakes are high!' By all accounts Billy was serious about his warning. It was like something out of a western movie.

In Annfield Plain, County Durham, when we played Castles Club, I got up one day leaving Jet in bed and thought that I'd go over the road to the pub for a drink. When I came to pay, the landlord said, 'That'll be £7.' Jet had been over before me and opened a slate! At the hotel, we got presented with the bill and we'd been having everything. We had no money and were past ourselves, but Hal Carter paid it. Backstage at Castles, one of the Dallas Boys got his old Rupert out and one of the Vernons – she was Welsh – said, 'I thought it was a microphone.'

When we played Castles, we stayed at the Washington Posthouse Hotel. One afternoon, while Hal was holding court, Jet sent him the same type of note that he'd once sent to Cliff Richard when he was talking with Alma Cogan in the Lotus House restaurant on Edgware Road, asking him to close his flies as he was upsetting other guests. Hal didn't let it disturb his composure.

Last year, at a Christmas show at the Isle of Wight's Medina Theatre, Jet came on as Santa Claus with, 'Bah, humbug, fiddlesticks, merry-bloody-Christmas!' Then, fingering his whiskers, he said, 'There's a hair in my mouth...that brings back memories!' Cliff Hall, in particular, was creased and could hardly play.

P.J. Proby

PERFORMER AND FELLOW EX-ALCOHOLIC

There are parallels between Jet and myself. I started off as Jett Powers and got my name when I signed with Gabbe, Lutz, Heller in Hollywood. Those were my first managers when I was 17, and they looked after the likes of Liberace, Kay Starr and Frankie Laine. They said they would have to change my name from Jimmy Smith because there was already a John Smith in the picture business. So they said, 'Think of a name.' Well, I liked a new picture, *Giant,* in which Jimmy Dean's name was 'Jett Rink', so I chose 'Jett' with two t's from that, and I also chose the name 'Towers'. So, I was Jett Towers for a few hours! Then they called me around four o'clock at the hotel and said, 'You've got to change your name from 'Towers' because we just signed a girl called Connie Towers, and it's her real name.' And so I thought, *Well... Tyrone Power...so what about 'Powers'?* So, I was Jett Powers from 1957 till 1962.

I arrived in the UK on March 15th, 1964 to be on the Beatles' first spectacular, *Around The Beatles.* It was their first big TV show to be shown all over the world, via satellite, and I think that we recorded it with Jack Good for the BBC at Wood Green in London. I was the only American on the show, along with the dancers from *West Side Story.* They were flown in from New York; I was flown in from California. The rest were newcomers on the scene like Cilla Black, Millie, Long John Baldry – and I think Joe Brown was on it, or supposed to be on it, because that's where I first met Joe, at rehearsals. And that's how everything started.

The Beatles had just come back from the *Ed Sullivan Show* in New York and 'I Want To Hold Your Hand' was No.1 in the USA, and it went to No.1 all over the world. The Telstar satellite hadn't been long out. Just as Elvis was the first rock'n'roller on television in 1953-54, the Beatles were the first group ever to be televised by Telstar all over the world. Years later I went back to Wood Green and swept streets.

I had majored in British History at school and just took the English peasant look when I came over here because I didn't have any clothes. I'd had to steal a shirt from Warner Brothers – it was Paul Newman's from *The Left Handed Gun.* I decided on the hair and the ponytail because of hygienic reasons, and the fact that English sailors used to wear it like that for the same reason. Also, I wanted to do something different. Elvis was famous for the pompadour with hair slicked back, ducktail and his sideburns, and the Beatles were famous for their hair in the face right down at the front. So I was the first one ever to wear a ponytail, just as the Beatles were the first ones to wear the mop-top and Elvis the sideburns.

I really didn't think much of the *talent* over here in this country, because I'd always heard it in America from the *real* people that put things out. When I came over here, everybody was covering records in the States. There was no real, live English music, and to me even the Shadows were like a copy of an American group. I didn't think the Beatles or anybody were gonna make it, because I didn't think that groups over here could ever hold down a big career like all of us solo singers – Elvis, Frank Sinatra and everybody. And, if you were gonna be in a group you gotta sound like the Ames Brothers, the Four Lads or the Four Preps – those groups in America. It was just like John Lennon – I told John that the Beatles were shit, and I told him, 'You'll last one year, and I'll take over.' His reply to me was, 'Well, if anybody takes over from us, Jim, I hope it's you.' So, we were all friends – I liked everybody – but I was *not* impressed by the talent in England *at all*!

I met Jet in 1964-65 at one of the nightclubs we all used to go to – either the Scotch of St James or the Ad-Lib, something like that. A couple of times I had to take him over my shoulder upstairs to his and Billie's apartment house and dump him off at the door, and Billie would take him in. Their flat was right above the Lotus House Chinese restaurant where Arthur Howes, the

P.J., early '60s.

agent and promoter, would hold meetings and eat. I knew Jet before I knew Billie, who I met through Diana Dors.

Jet looked a bit like James Dean in those days with that big, floppy blond hair. It only got yellow and yellower as he got more and more into the drink and everything, and the hair colour didn't help him stay out of fights. What I liked about Jet was that he was my type of person. He wasn't afraid of a street fight: he was a street man and a real drinking hellraiser. If I said, 'Let's go to the Queen's Stables and take the horses at three or four in the morning, and go and ride them through Hyde Park,' he was not against any of that.

When we were together he never mentioned his first wife

or anything like that. In fact, we never even talked about any kind of business. We just talked about the person that was in front of us and what we were gonna do that night, and what we were gonna do next. I never talked about Hollywood or Elvis, or anything like that, and he never talked about Cliff, the Shadows or anything. I was just with whoever was around at the moment in the nightclub. It could be Jet, Screaming Lord Sutch – it was whoever came in and sat down at the table with me. I never kept in contact with anybody. Unless I saw them on the night, I never saw anybody; I never ran around with people. People came over to my house in their cars, usually after the pubs and clubs closed, simply because it was the only place in London that they could find a drink. I ran a wet bar there all the time.

Like Jet, my parents introduced me to alcohol. When we used to have the barbecues in Texas they would say, 'Give the little boy a drink,' and of course they'd give me a slug of beer. And I would do funny dances and everything and they'd say, 'He's really funny, give him another swig.' I never really got into the hard stuff until I came here to England.

I did sign with Robert Stigwood when I first came over to the UK to do a tour with the Rolling Stones and people like that, but we had a little tiff and set-to about the contract and he cancelled the whole tour. That was in 1964 when I was living at Ennismore Mews in Hyde Park right off from Kensington. I lived there for about a year and then moved to Chelsea, right across the road from the Duke of Wellington's Barracks. Ringo now lives right next door to where I used to live. So, with no management and having to deal myself with the top brass like Lew and Leslie Grade, and the Delfonts, and these big men who ran the business, I was having to have Dutch courage and that's when I started drinking the hard stuff.

After Jet and Billie's car accident, neither one of them could get a job, so his depression was actually because of the fact that he couldn't get work anywhere. He'd been replaced in that group with Cliff Richard and now his solo career was halted. His drinking didn't help him, but he went back to work too soon. He had a very, very serious wound and the hospital didn't treat him for such. They just dumped him. He and Billie came very near to death in that crash, and the hospital treated him in the emergency room and then – out! Billie had a broken jaw and a broken neck; she had a broken everything, and she still has problems with it all today. They just put a Band-Aid on both of them and let 'em go. Jet discharged himself, but there are ways to keep you in. When he did receive it, his compensation from the accident was very poor.

I didn't have as much of a problem with alcohol as Jet did, because I could work under alcohol; Jet couldn't. My trouble with a bad boy image, created by the press, was mostly caused by Mary Whitehouse and Lord Longford after the pants-splitting incident. That happened at the Fairfield Halls, Croydon. After – it might have been at Luton – they didn't allow me to go onstage, and they had to put Tom Jones on. I was banned from the Odeons, the Ranks – nearly all theatres – and everything that had to do with teenagers, I was not allowed in. I really don't have a clue how they could have enforced that, and I've never really known.

I've been dry for twelve years now since I gave it up in 1992. I'm 66 now and I'll never touch booze again. When I was 65, I think Jet was over at my house and I think we had a couple of cans of orange juice or something. I was into some non-alcoholic beer with added nutrients, etc, till someone said that it was really bad for you.

I understand perfectly what he went through. He wasn't drunk all the time. People mistook him for being drunk when he was upset. When he went around with a shotgun, got thrown into jail for being drunk and all that kind of stuff, it wasn't alcohol that was coming out. It was the depression, and being upset at either something that had happened that day between him and a loved one, or upset and depressed about show business in general and what was happening to his life.

Jet's a nice guy, and nice guys do depend on ladies and everything like that, but nobody has ever portrayed me like that. In fact, they don't think that I've changed at all. Most people think that I'm dead. When I go onstage, I think the only reason I draw a crowd is that people just come to make sure I'm alive, 'cause my friend, Sharon Sheeley, put it around in the papers many, many years ago that I was dead when I was living up in the Pennines in Charlotte Brontë's barn at Haworth. I built an apartment house – a kind of hidey-bunk type thing – out of her barn, which is right across from the Brontë Parsonage. And I stayed up there for a few years and nobody knew where I was, so I can see why people woulda thought I was dead.

I haven't been allowed to tour in this country for forty years. Since 2002 – when I went on tour with the Searchers – until this day is the only time I've been allowed to work the circuit in this country because of the bad publicity. The fact that it was that long didn't change things for me. It never changed anything. Most of all the agents died. They've all gone now, but the people that replaced them just kept the same attitude – up until now. I was allowed to work on the stage in plays, and in nightclubs. But nightclubs have been gone now for over 20-30 years. They were really flourishing when I was having to play nightclubs – places like Batley Variety Club, which was just like Las Vegas, and the Top Hat, Spennymoor, County Durham, La Dolce Vita, Newcastle and the Fiesta in Stockton. They were beautiful places and the pay was great, but the minute they turned them into discos, they never had a chance of becoming nightclubs again.

When the club scene died around the beginning of the '80s, there was absolutely no place for me. I didn't have anywhere to do music. Clubs were better than one-nighters: they used to hire us for seven days. We'd be on one venue for seven nights. That doesn't happen anymore. Sometimes, we'd even do two shows a night by 'doubling up' at another club – and that would be for the same pay, but a shorter set.

There were other artists on besides us. There were tons of comedians. I remember being on with Frank Carson and Jimmy Tarbuck – they were just starting off. In those days, they could get such acts cheap before they got national exposure on television. When I came over to England, television went off at eleven o'clock at night, and it was only black & white TV;

colour didn't come in until '65-'66. We'd never heard of such a thing in America. We were used to all-night television since the mid-'50s.

Just yesterday I was up in Spennymoor because I was playing a concert a few miles away. I went and I saw some old friends like John Ray, who used to own the Top Hat and Spennymoor Variety Club. And, boy, we just chewed over everything and he's coming to my show at Durham City tomorrow. John's a big agent now, but they don't book nightclubs anymore – there aren't any. The working men's clubs will always be there.

Jet and I are both animal-lovers and I know that both he and Billie are into cats. I'm looking into the eyes of my dog, Tilly, who's here in bed right next to me. She's all red and a cross between Billie Davis's dog, which was a dachshund, and a Jack Russell. So, she's long and near the floor like a dachshund, but she's got the temperament of a Jack Russell and brings me ten dead rabbits in a day, plus rats and mice. She's a terror: she thinks she's a damned Rotweiller!

Both Jet and I have been criticised in our career, but I always remember what Elvis Presley told me. He said, 'If anybody knocks me or anything, I just look at the shape of their head and feel sorry for them.' This was probably because Elvis considered the shape of his head to be perfection. He always used to talk about his Cadillac nose, his Cadillac hair and his Cadillac face, and that he drove a Cadillac car. Everything to Elvis was a Cadillac, so it was, 'Look at those people, they haven't got a Cadillac head.'

Like Jet, I leaned on women for many years, too. I had six wives, and it's only since 1993 that I haven't had a wife and have been learning to live and do everything on my own. And I'm still in a learning process. They've all been young – 16 to 23 – never any older than that. They wrapped me around their fingers, and I just moulded them in the way that I lived. I don't come across temptation as much since I'm not drinking anymore. I had a lot of time on my hands when I got married in the old days. Thank the Lord, I don't have that much time now.

Claudia Martin, Dean Martin's eldest daughter, and I were just about to get married when she sent me to jail for 3½ months for chasing her down Santa Monica Boulevard with a .45. We were going to have a double wedding with her father, but Dean said he didn't want to marry his lady, Cathy, who worked as a receptionist at the biggest hairdresser's in Beverly Hills, so he went his way and I rotted there in jail. Sadly, Claudia died of breast cancer.

I've never had any children. I had mumps when I was seven and it left me sterile. But I *like* children – I raised a bunch. I raised Claudia Martin's child. Her name was Jessie. When I married Judy Howard – the recent film *Seabiscuit* was about the Howard family – she already had a daughter, Brigitte. So, I've been used to raising children, but never fathered any.

My family are nearly all gone now. On my mother's side, there's an Uncle Dan left, he's 95. And on my father's side, there's my Uncle Joe, he's about 92. And that's about the end of it, everybody's gone.

Jet, Billie and I are still good friends. Billie's raised a big family of her own and I'm friends with her daughter and her son, as I've known her children since they were six or seven years old and they're teenagers now. She still cares about Jet and a lot of people, and it's probably why she hasn't gone far in this dog-eat-dog business – she's too nice. Robert Stigwood let everybody go when he signed the Bee Gees and just concentrated on them. Everyone else in the stable was not worked at all. He just had a group that he was going to make into the next Beatles and he didn't have time for anybody else – including Billie.

That's why I didn't sign with the Beatles' manager, Brian Epstein. He wanted me to sign with him, but I said no. I said, 'I've been with Colonel Parker and watched how he runs Elvis, and I know through what I've seen that you only have time for one artist, and that's the Beatles. Everybody else'll just stick on the shelf. So, I'll just carry on as I am.'

The down days and humiliations got to me the same as they got to Jet, but I had a tougher hide 'cause I came out of Hollywood, where it's really rough. Jet did a variety of jobs to survive, and I was a street cleaner in London right outside the theatres where I used to perform onstage. I just did odd jobs like helping people raise their cattle and sheep up in the North of England, and helping with the hay when it needed to be brought in.

It's really great to see Jet doing things again, because, like me, he went through a long, long period of time of idleness and no one would touch him.

Now, I'm working – like Jet – constantly. And that's like a kind-of change for the both of us. Once you've got a fan market out there, age doesn't come into it; they're with you for life. Jet'll have his people that will go to see him for the rest of his life. They probably relate to the tragic side because they have it in their normal lives. And it's not really supposed to hit entertainers. We're supposed to be bulletproof, and if you're not bulletproof, then we kinda become one of theirs. Mine was more magnified because I was a rebel outlaw cowboy from the United States with a Texas accent. Mine came more from a Hollywood side. I didn't pay attention to the Establishment; I was just paying attention to having a good time.

Cliff Richard

PERFORMER

I hadn't seen Jet around before the 1958 autumn Kalin Twins tour. I'm not quite sure whether he'd toured before that, or whether that was the first big time for all of us. I know that for Hank, Bruce and I, it was our first tour as such, ever. Jet may have toured with others, I don't know.

The first time I met him would probably have been on the coach. We all used to meet outside the Planetarium in London's Baker Street and used to get on a bus there. I remember the first time I ever went on tour – that was the first bus ride I ever took that I didn't feel sick on, to be honest with you. We all met outside; we would definitely have met him then and we would've all shared the bus and started the tour right there. I didn't know him from the Vipers; in fact, the Vipers were going then, but I wasn't into skiffle as such. The Vipers were like Lonnie Donegan, who had come just a little bit before people like myself and probably coincided with Tommy Steele, who came about a year or so before I did.

Jet was actually playing for the Most Brothers, but he sat in on our sessions 'cause he liked what we were doing; and that's how, in fact, when we came towards the end of the tour, we asked him to join us as bass player. Jet played for a number of people on the tour, but used to sit in for me. In fact, I always think that Hank played guitar for somebody else, and they all made so much more money than I did! I may have been on £200 a week, but I had to pay them as well out of that £200 – and my manager, John Foster. I think I got ten quid a week!

Jet's recollection of me in my pink jacket asking him to join us, and him turning it down, and then him approaching me later in the tour after talking to Arthur Howes and learning that 'Move It' was in the charts, it's pretty close.

We were listening to him playing for the Most Brothers, and because he was sitting in on my set and playing as well a couple of times during that tour – I don't know whether he remembers that – but playing bass for us 'cause he just enjoyed our music, it felt good. 'Cause like the other guys, they weren't unique in that there were other bands playing really well, but they were unique in that their gel was so different and in that respect they were kinda ahead of everybody else, and they had personalities. And, as you know, Jet was a great-looking guy. He's the first guy I ever met who had dyed his hair blond. So, he looked great, and Hank looked distinctive. When they played together it created a sound, and it was magic when they did. So it was a pretty obvious choice for us, and then of course he and Bruce and Hank remembered jamming at the 2I's with a drummer called Tony Meehan, and that's how we got the fourth member eventually.

Ian Samwell was actually a guitarist and played a bit of bass for us on that tour, but it was obviously not how it could finish, and in fact it was pretty obvious that we couldn't cope with the drummer either. My drummer, Terry Smart, was a really nice guy and played on 'Move It', but couldn't seem to hit it when it came to different arrangements and stuff. And we had a great chat, 'cause he was a good school friend of mine and it was very painful for me, but it was obvious that I couldn't actually move forward unless I had a really great band with me. So, I asked Jet to join us and Ian began to get more involved as a writer really. In fact, we had a couple of big hits with his stuff after that.

They didn't have long to gel, but sometimes in rock'n'roll there doesn't need to be if you've all got the same aim. They all seemed to like the same kind of pop-rock music as I did, and so it was easy for me to head them because they enjoyed doing what I was doing, and I *loved* what they were doing. So, it was the perfect gel and, as you know, it was a fact that we were a *tour de force* here because they had hit records. And if they weren't No.1, then chances are I would be, and we often pushed each other off the No.1 slot.

We had great power when we went out on tour, and it's

just as well that happened, 'cause when the Beatles came along of course everyone swung towards the Beatles. The one thing that saved my mind was that we were still selling out concerts and selling our records. We were still having No.1s, and so I tried to be philosophical about it and say, 'Well, okay, we're still here; we're still surviving. The Beatles haven't wiped us out.' It was partly because we were a terrific team together, and I think we created something that even the Beatles couldn't really take away from us – ever. And they never did of course.

When we did the 1960 season at the Palladium in *Stars In Your Eyes* with Russ Conway, Joan Regan, Edmund Hockridge and David Kossoff, although the Shadows had the No.1 record in the country with 'Apache' during the run, they weren't allowed to play it because they were not featured on that show in their own right. It could never happen nowadays. Any producer of a show would say, 'Crikey, we've got the No.1! Let's slot them in somewhere.'

I just remember it being great fun in those days, and it *had* to be fun. We lived on a big blue bus and we spent the whole time touring; it was just unbelievable, month after month. It was fun, and if you didn't enjoy it, it would've been murderous; it would've killed us. But fortunately we just loved the whole aspect of being new at it, and successful – really successful – at it too, and having kids screaming at us all over the place. It's indescribable. It was just fantastic. So, I can understand why he still remembers it with relish, and I do too.

Jet was an impish sort of guy: he was always faffing around and messing around. I must admit, I'm never quite sure why the Shadows didn't stick together longer, because they still had so much more to offer. Even now, the Shadows, when they go on tour, they have such success that it's incredible to think that they are now planning to do their final farewell tour of Europe, and I'm sure there'll be a comeback as well. But in those days...I don't know whether it was unique – it is difficult to use the word 'unique' anymore because so many people go through the same thing and we just didn't know other people were going through it – but certainly onstage we had great fun.

Oh Boy! 1958.
Left to right: Cliff, Jet, Terry Smart and Bruce Welch.

Jet was the quiet one onstage. He was described by Jack Good as 'the mean, moody and magnificent one of the band', and it was Hank and Bruce and I who did all the chatter and banter at the front, but offstage he wasn't quiet, and he had this huge thing about photography as well. He was heavily into photography and all sorts of things. We seemed to all get on together really well, too, I seem to remember.

What amazes me is that when it finally did happen, when we split, it wasn't because I split with the Shadows; it was the Shadows who broke up. And I suddenly found that the band had disintegrated and they all wanted to do different things. In a way, as time goes by, you realise that's what happens to musicians. They want to try their own thing; they want to write their own music, or play their own instrumental, and not have to rely on someone else. And with a band you do have to agree how that final piece of music comes out.

Me working with strings, or my management pushing me into a different style, had nothing to do with it, as I did that way back in 1961-62. I recorded with Norrie Paramor's orchestra on my third and fourth album, I think it was. So, I had already started doing that anyway. No, they're the ones who broke up. If you hear anything different, that's definitely wrong. You can write it if you like, but it'll be wrong.

They're the ones that wanted to do different things and there were personality clashes between a couple of them. So, I guess it happens to bands; it happened to the Beatles. And the funny thing is, it happened to the Shadows after ten years, and it seems like the Beatles got about ten years before they all did their own thing. It seems to be a pattern that happens with bands.

I was disappointed at first, but fortunately again, you see, I think, in terms of my longevity, one of the best things that happened to me was that Norrie Paramor said, 'Let's go and record orchestral music just to make the album sound different.' It gave me a taste of working with other musicians. So, when the band left, although I felt slightly empty, I thought, 'My goodness, what am I going to do now?' At least I'd made a couple of tracks without them, and so I went into the studio with musicians that I'd met before. We didn't have the same relationship, of course. That was never gonna be the same, but at least I got a chance to work with other people and was able to continue my career.

You know, rock'n'roll the way we did it would be considered 'middle of the road' now. It was basic music: very 'live', and recorded in mono when we first started. I have always been a pop-rock singer; that's what it is. And, if people give titles to it, 'middle of the road' kinda means that you tend to appeal to a middle group of people – which is the *largest* group of course. I'm happy with that, but every now and then you can divert and go off into another direction if you wish. But part of that came because Norrie had pushed me into working with other people, so I was happy in whatever situation I found myself in eventually. But at first it was not nice. I didn't like it when I was in the studio and the Shadows weren't there.

I didn't even think about 'the dyed-blond-haired, drinking and smoking and womanising Mr Harris'. Now you mention it, I suppose all those things were going on amongst all the people on the tour at that particular time, but now of course I realise that what I thought was herbal was probably pot being smoked backstage. I'm not saying for one minute that Jet smoked pot – I wouldn't have known that.

I never smoked. I couldn't stay in the room when they did smoke. I used to really hate it. And I still find it very uncomfortable sitting amongst people that smoke, because it just irritates my throat, irritates my nostrils, and irritates my brain because, in fact, I might get cancer from something they're enjoying. So, I always used to either not be in the room, or just try to be as far away from it as possible.

I hate to say it, but I think Jet's problem was that he did end up with a huge problem with drink, but he dealt with that and I think that's great.

I didn't have a word with him at the time. I don't think I would have had a word with anybody at that stage because we were all so young. To have a word with someone you need to have had some sort of *experience*. For me, it was just something that, for instance, my father had always done. My father always smoked incredibly heavily, and so I was used to having smokers around, but I never, ever liked it, ever. So, I would never take it upon myself to advise him.

The same with drink. Of course we all drank a little, didn't we? He did use to drink a bit. Rather than give advice, we used to say, 'But you can't go and drink and come on drunk, it's not fair on the rest of us.' So, he must have heard that a number of times from both the band and from Tito Burns!

I hope that I'm saying the right thing here: I think Jet told me that he'd been an alcoholic and got over it all. So, once you've got that on the agenda, you don't have a choice: you have to drink, or you cut it right out. It took him a heck of a long time to do that and, of course, in a way it ended his career with the Shadows. It was one of the main reasons why they couldn't work with him anymore. You can understand: you can't have people falling about on the stage when you're presenting a two-hour show with all the necessary concentration. It's damaging everything, and most important, it was damaging him. At least he's done it now and it hasn't killed him.

Jet's drinking didn't cause me any particular embarrassment either on or off the stage when he worked with me. I think it was more when they went off separately and did things that things went wrong. I mean, I heard stories about him being so drunk onstage he could barely stand and things like that. One of them was at the Cavern, when they pushed him back onstage again. That never happened with me; I'm glad it didn't actually. He never embarrassed me socially either. He was very, very easy to be with: very chatty, very funny. We used to sit around the coach and rabbit and chat and laugh together, end up late somewhere in a bar – well, no, bars didn't stay open late in those days, but certainly in a hotel room. And we had guys that worked for us on the merchandise that were very funny and we used to all get together, laugh, gag around, and sing and stuff. So, he was an easy character to be with. The drinking stuff must've really steamrollered after they kinda split with me I think.

We used to discuss him, obviously, and say, 'Look, I don't know how we can cope with this.' We were all so young – I guess none of us really knew how to deal with it. In fact, at that stage, there's no way I would've thought he was an alcoholic; just thought he drank too much. I think that things have changed now. I know that if that ever happened in my band, I would certainly have them aside and go through things with them. But I'm a man now; I was a boy then.

I don't want to say anything about Jet's marriage because I've dealt with this already in my autobiography and I don't intend to talk about personal things ever, ever again to be honest with you, either about my family or my friends. So, sorry about that.

I have great respect for our manager, Peter Gormley. Peter was the one guy that we could all go and talk to, and we did. Maybe Jet should have gone and talked to him. Peter was very much a man of: 'You live your life. If you wanna get married,

you get married. If you don't wanna record that, you don't record it. If you don't wanna do this, tell me and we won't do it.' But he didn't enforce anything. He must have had to at some point – at some point talked to Jet. Chronologically, I'm not quite sure how long Jet overlapped with Peter Gormley.

I know that Jet was part of the band when Tito Burns was my manager. The Shadows had already made 'Apache', and I was still with Tito Burns, and I asked Peter Gormley to manage me. I had to wait for my contract to finish, so I think Peter took over in 1962 or something like that.

I think it's really hard to say who was the leader of the group. It was obvious from the very beginning though that the leader of the band, from the public's point of view, was Hank. Because when you're the lead guitarist, that's all people hear. People hear the backing, but they're not aware of it, because if they're listening to the man playing 'Apache', that's the man who leads the band. And in every respective case, in fact, that is the man who leads the band. But they were all so good at what they did, you know. Everybody knows that the drummer is the *spine* any band that there is. You don't have a good drummer; you don't have a good band. So they were all as you say 'first amongst equals', but I never thought of anybody actually being the leader of the band.

We all did things together; we all argued and barneyed about the kind of sounds that we wanted on our records. We all said, 'Nah, I don't like that, try something else.' So, there was no leader as such. Maybe there should've been, I don't know. I only ever dealt with the Shadows in terms of music, and that was the mainstay of our lives at that time; that's what really counted. I wouldn't have gone to them on anything else. It was run as a democracy, that's what I'm saying. Maybe that's why bands break up, because in the end everybody has an opinion and wants that opinion to be the forefront of things, and once that doesn't happen it can cause friction.

I was always very happy with the way things sounded when we were together. I don't remember having too many big arguments in the studio. I remember that we used to get all the arguments done with at rehearsal periods. We used to read about the Beatles going into a studio for four days and they hadn't even got a song written. We would have our songs written and rehearsed and then go to the studio merely to record. So, we were probably one of the cheapest bands that were successful that EMI ever had, because the cost of the studio is ginormous.

And so we would have all our arguments in Jet's apartment, or mine, or wherever we would be rehearsing. One or the other would say, 'It should be something...'. Bruce would say, 'No, no, I think it should be a waltz.' Somebody else would say, 'No, no, it should be this.' We would get rid of all of that during rehearsals, and when we got to the studio it was just a matter of concentrating on getting it right. And in those days we did record live, you know. If anybody did it wrong, you always had to do the whole darn thing again. So, it was pretty concentrated stuff.

I don't remember ever saying anything to any of them about bum notes. If Jet had played a bum note, I wouldn't have heard him for the screaming. Nowadays, I have an in-ear sound system in my head; in those days I'd just stand in the middle and there'd be a blast from behind me. Bruce might have heard it, but I'd be thinking about what I was doing. You have to have a pretty bad bum note, and I don't remember it happening. Of course, the bass can be a very deceiving instrument onstage. Nowadays, maybe it's more exposed, but in those days it was far more of a *feel*, and if he had hit a bum note or two I wouldn't have noticed, I don't think.

Bruce was the one who was probably more concerned about our image in terms of what people saw onstage. I know he used to always arrive an hour and half to two hours earlier just to watch the amplifiers and the guitars; just to make sure that they looked good. And so any disturbance to that perfection would have absolutely upset Bruce horrifically. Of course I know, having worked with him as a producer, he's the same way about bum notes from musicians on the studio floor as well. He was very particular about that. So, yeah, I was aware that he would've been the one. And, of course, sometimes Jet probably may not have been able to deal with the way Bruce dealt with him, because Bruce would've been very, very strong about things like that.

You have to remember, in those days we were the first of a kind. Well, there were two or three of us: Marty Wilde & His Wildcats, the Tornados. We were kinda seen as the first because we were the first real big act that came out like that. And so, therefore, for an agent, they would've thought, *Oh, it's the singer, it's the singer.* In the same way as when I was first asked to go and sing up North in a ballroom, we were called 'The Drifters'. And they wanted a name in front. I said, 'No, no, "The Drifters".' They said, 'No, we want a name.' So I found my name; that's how 'Cliff Richard' was discovered – the name – and it became Cliff Richard & The Drifters. That's the way people felt: the singer had to be the prominent issue. So, an agent – it's understandable when you look back – they thought, *Well, it's just a band. If we have any trouble we'll get four other guys.* And, of course, Tito Burns was an old-style manager and agent.

After that, the Shadows took off in their own right. I did

whatever I could. In fact, in terms of promotion for that first record, we used my name and just to get me there legitimately, I actually played an Indian tom-tom thing and I start the track of 'Apache': *chuck-chuck-chuck-chuck.* It's silly, that's all I played on it. I think that, and the end. And it was, 'Oh, Cliff Richard plays on the first record by his group.'

But for me – again, maybe I was a bit wiser than I can remember being, but I remember thinking that, if the Shadows have hits, then the girls can come and see me, and the guys would go and see Hank and the boys. And if we're both on together, we're never gonna be short of a full house. So, for me it was a good business move to do it. Also we got on so well; we were friends, and I thought it was a unique thing that a singer and a band should be swapping places at No.1 in the charts, which is what we did for a number of years, you know. Yeah, I did stick up for them.

I didn't go out to bat for them with Norrie Paramor to get them a recording contact; that would've been Peter Gormley. Peter was very heavily involved with Frank Ifield as well at the time and was very good friends with Norrie. He knew my band, of course, and I think it would've come up more as his idea.

When Norrie mentioned that he was going to work with the Shadows, I thought it was fantastic. I mean, I would *never* have stood in the way. I couldn't have done anyway, could I, really? I think they were too good; they would've done it anyway. As I say, I'd rather have been part of it than not be part of it; because when I think now, it was a major part of my career. I hope that they feel that way about me, because it is a sort-of fact that, if I hadn't started then, maybe they would never have met. I found Bruce and Hank; we asked Jet to join us, and Tony Meehan, and so I played a part in the creation of that band. So, I felt a part of it even though I never was. Even when they did their own things, I still felt like, *Oh, it's my band.*

It wasn't difficult really, having to separate from the guys after a show because of the fans; it was a pragmatic thing. People were screaming at me and it was obviously a 'love affair', but it can be dangerous and so, therefore, I used to be hustled out quietly. But I used to like the times in the very early days; we always used a blue Thames van that we escaped in. Particularly I remember in Blackpool we used to get in the back of this van and all be driven out together.

We really loved that van. When the Beatles first got started, we were in the same theatre and they came and did a Sunday night concert there and had no way of getting out. They were totally unfamiliar with the situation and we lent them our van. I wonder if they ever remember that one. But it wasn't difficult, it was just the fact of saying, 'You go out this way...'

Again, funnily enough, I've made jokes about the fact that I used to write with the Shadows at one time, and then suddenly I found them saying to me things like, 'You're the star of the show, you go and do the press conference.'

Now, I exaggerated a little bit, but I've said that when I used to get back to the hotel they had a whole new album written, and they'd done it without me. I used to think the album was terrific and I enjoyed singing their songs. So, in the same way, things like that happening, where we were separated because the girls were screaming at me and stuff; in fact, in a way, I'm sure what they thought to themselves was, 'Let Cliff go out that way, they'll all go rushing round there. We can walk quietly to the pub.'

I was kept informed of developments regarding Jet. I knew, of course, that he was going to leave and I kind-of knew why, because of his condition onstage. I was disappointed, but life has to go on, and I guess we have to deal with that sort of thing. I think it was probably the best thing for Jet that ever happened too, because he did go off and do a couple of fantastic records; and then dealt with his problem as well – which is far more important, I guess. I still feel that the best thing he's ever done in his life was to kick drink.

I didn't try to stop him leaving and I don't think I would've done it. At that stage, too, remember, we were all having our own hits and we were our own men. And in a way, although it affected me, it was much more of an effect for them. They made all those decisions for themselves. When Tony Meehan left, again there was a discrepancy of understanding between them; Tony left and Brian Bennett came in.

I'm not surprised that Jet surfaced quickly after leaving, but, you know, Jack Good is a man who can see ahead a little and say that this guy has potential for this and this guy has potential for that. In a way, that's what he did with me. He's the one that stopped me looking like Elvis and said, 'You've got to do something else.' And because of his work with me on TV, I became a kind of performer that was different. So, it doesn't surprise me that Jet would go for advice and get it, and get good stuff too. You must remember that people liked Jet. People enjoyed him onstage, and he looked *great*, so he had a female following too.

Chris Tremlett

JET'S AUNTY CHRIS

Our mother had seven children: two girls and five boys. Wyn, Terry's mother, was the first child, but she was born out of wedlock, which in those days was a source of great shame. As a result, she was brought up by grandparents. She was lucky in one way because they were well off, whereas our mother and father with six additional children were not. When our mother got pregnant, one of my brothers used to say to me, 'Not another baby!'

Wyn, who was ten years older than me, had Terry in 1939, so I've known him since he was born and we've always kept in touch throughout his life. By the time he was about nine or ten months old, I was going round to see him regularly and, as Wyn had to go back to work at Hall Telephones in Willesden, I started to look after him. I was 15 and Terry was one year old when I used to take him out in a pram with his gas mask on. He was a beautiful boy with blue eyes and blond hair. In his teenage years he had alopecia and his hair grew back in brown.

Wyn would often bring him round to mum's and I would take him out a lot. I don't know why. His mum and dad didn't neglect him; I just liked spending time with him. Sometimes we all went out together. Wyn was a bit strict with him. Terry was never spoiled, but he was never shown a lot of affection. But I know that Wyn loved him, and so did Bill.

I can remember Saturday afternoons in particular, when Wyn and Bill and another couple they were friendly with went to the speedway and I looked after Terry. Sometimes, I used to sleep over at Wyn and Bill's house and look after him. Wyn was lovely, but she never showed her love or feelings. I took him to the pictures when he was about four years old and the film was set in a boys' school. One of the characters was called Inky and, young as he was, every time we went to the pictures for some time after that he used to say that he wanted to see Inky again.

I was delighted when he went into music and became successful at something he loved doing. Before they got together with Cliff Richard properly, Bruce Welch, Hank Marvin and Terry came to Wyn and Bill's home and we all went around looking for rooms they could rent.

Carol Costa told me about her feelings for Cliff Richard before the wedding. She was a very 'funny' girl and not the type of girl I thought he'd marry. I didn't dislike her. She looked like Brigitte Bardot and seemed quite genuine, but she was bossy and he was so easy-going then.

When they wanted to get married, Terry would be nearly 19 and Carol just 17, so they needed parental consent. I think that Carol's parents were okay about it, but not Wyn and Bill, so they came to see us to sign the necessary consent papers. Terry always came to talk to Arthur and me. We told him that we couldn't do as he was asking, that we'd never go against Wyn and Bill like that, and that he should talk it over with them again, which he did.

Theirs was a white wedding in June 1959, but I can't remember on which Saturday. I think it must have been early on in the month as my birthday is 29 June and I would have remembered if it had been Saturday the 27th.

Carol's behaviour with Cliff Richard definitely caused Terry's drinking in the first place, and the accident that he and Billie suffered just accelerated it. He was definitely not a born alcoholic. I think that the other Shadows let him down and could have been more supportive. Years later, Ricky, Terry's son by Carol, once turned up when he was doing a show and the lad looked like Cliff Richard in my opinion.

When Terry became successful with the Shadows and had money, he was always very generous and it was 'drinks all round'. In fact, he used to give his money away to anyone who asked or needed it. Terry's had some lovely women. Patti Brook, who he went out with after he and Carol split up, was a lovely girl, but he treated her very badly. He brought Billie Davis to see my husband and I. She was a very smart girl and came all dressed in black. Black cape, black sombrero, black skirt and boots and sweeping false eyelashes that you could have dusted the room with. My husband used to say that she was like the Sandeman's Port advertising man. Billie had an uncle and an aunt, and the uncle was a golf professional at a club. We used to visit them and Billie's uncle gave my Arthur a set of clubs; he was over the moon.

When he lived with Billie and was up in court for holding up people with an empty gun, the police phoned Wyn and Bill as they wanted to keep the weapon. They referred them on to Terry and in the end Terry let them keep the gun. He was never a violent person.

It upset Wyn and Bill greatly when he started to drink. We all used to go down to see Jet, Maggie, his third wife, and the children when they lived in a caravan. On one occasion, Bill got so upset with Terry's drunken behaviour towards Maggie and said, 'That's it! I've had it with you.' Next day, Terry came to our hotel chatting to us and picking food off our plates. He couldn't remember what he'd been like the day before.

When Wyn became a widow and lived in St Osyth's in Clacton, Essex, we bought a caravan down there and often visited her and Terry, who was still living with Maggie. Terry was into photography then and used to take photos of rainbows and lightning. He is an excellent photographer and made his living as one. We had that caravan for years. I only sold it last year, and still regret doing it.

When he lived in Gloucester with his mum, after he split up with Jackie, me and my brother Fred used to go and see him and take tobacco and give him money. Wyn said not to give him money, as he'd use it to buy drink, but in spite of her warning I used to slip him a fiver. It was wrong of me I know, but I couldn't bear to see him stuck. Terry and Wyn came to our house one Christmas and I had to hide the alcohol and give him non-alcoholic drinks. His system couldn't stand the non-alcohol and on the way home he was desperately searching for pubs. Eventually he found one and downed two pints to steady himself. It used to hurt me a great deal to see him like that. Terry is my favourite nephew and we have always had a close bond, which was made even stronger because I was unable to have any children myself. All through his life we have kept in touch, and I am so proud and pleased that he is now sober and still performing so brilliantly.

Bruce Welch

MUSICIAN

Ah yes, the Vitapointe Kid! Hank and I met Jet in the 2I's not long after we arrived in London in April of 1958. The James Dean look was 'in' and Jet styled himself to look like the film star who made such a big teenage impact with films like *Rebel Without A Cause* and *East Of Eden*. Both Hank and I were in awe of him and his experience, as at that time he was certainly one of the best musicians that I had come across. He could adapt his playing to any musical style, and as a consequence of such versatility he was always in demand. If a group needed a bass player, they sent for Jet Harris. We often played together onstage at the 2I's if we were hanging around at the same time, but nothing formal. Jet was always a character, but during those early days I can't recall whether he drank or not.

When Cliff & The Drifters – comprising Hank on lead guitar, Ian 'Sammy' Samwell on bass, Terry Smart on drums and me on rhythm guitar – toured with the Kalin Twins in October 1958, Jet was on the same bill backing the Most Brothers. During the tour Cliff asked him he would like to join the Drifters as a replacement for Ian Samwell. At the end of that year Tony Meehan replaced Terry Smart, and it was this new line-up of the Drifters which made its debut at Manchester's Free Trade Hall in January 1959. We were all different types, but good mates – as was Cliff, who never let the fact that he was our boss and paying our wages get in the way of genuine friendship. Hank and I liked partying and girls, but were never into drinking or 'jazz Woodbines'. I preferred a good cup of tea, but we all mixed well and I have great memories of those heady early days. Hank, Jet Tony and I were an amazing little band.

Early in 1959, Jet met Carol Costa and brought her backstage to meet Cliff, Hank, Tony and I at one of our shows.

Although very attractive in a sexy 'Brigitte Bardot' sort of way, Carol struck me as a very strong character. Jet, who was then easy-going, was clearly smitten and they married about five months later. Carol accompanied us on tour occasionally and quickly became part of our 'family'.

Cliff and Carol were obviously fond of each other right from the outset, but it never struck me that anything was going on at first because we were all such friends. Their relationship was always secret and never blatant. It became evident to me after Jet and Carol were married when Cliff and Carol had adjoining sleepers on a train from London to Blackpool. Jet was allocated a sleeper well away from Cliff and his wife! Why he allowed that to happen I don't know. The pressure of his wife's behaviour with his boss was too much for Jet in my opinion, and he attempted to cope by drinking.

It all seemed to come to a head during our six-month Palladium stint which started in June 1960, and by 1962 all the rows and recriminations led to divorce proceedings. Although we didn't like what was happening with Cliff and Carol, Hank, Tony and myself never broached the matter with Cliff. Perhaps we should have done, but we were all still in our teens and probably decided that it wasn't any of our business. At that time most of the girls in Britain were in love with Cliff Richard as he was *the* rock'n'roll star and, sadly for Jet, Carol was one of them. There was no doubt in our minds that Carol made the running and I think she scared Cliff to death.

As Jet's drinking got worse, it began to affect the Shadows' performance on occasions, and when he got himself into bar fights I started to nag him about the booze. We may have hit lucky in music business terms, but we were hard workers and wanted no bad press. Everything that Hank and I had dreamed of had come true and we didn't want anything to jeopardise our career and what we had achieved.

Sam Curtis, our road manager, saved Jet's bacon on many occasions when his drinking meant he was absent near to showtime, or it looked like his aggressive behaviour in a pub was going to earn him a beating. I had also pulled him out of similar

situations and we were all sick of it. Cliff may have made the odd comment, but left Jet to the rest of the Shadows and Sam Curtis. After all, following the success of 'Apache' in 1960 and a succession of massive hits, by this time we were not just Cliff's backing group; we were a big name in our own right.

Looking back with a lot more experience of life, I can see that my nagging him placed even more pressure on him and probably pushed up his alcohol consumption. But then we were young lads and none of us had any experience of alcoholics to seek the necessary help for Jet and, even if we had been that wise, he would have had to cooperate.

It all came to a head in early 1962 and Jet left the group. He maintains that he quit, but actually Hank and I – after several ultimatums – sacked him. Obviously no one 'owned' the Shadows group, as Hank, Jet and I at that time were a group of equals, so we couldn't legally sack him as an employer could. However, faced with a firm stance from both Hank and I, after several unheeded ultimatums, it was really impossible for him to continue as a Shadow, just as Tony Meehan's hand was forced in 1961 by Hank, Jet and I over different behaviour problems. With Hank, Jet, Tony and I, we had split everything equally four ways. When Tony left, Brian Bennett was taken on at a wage of £50 by the three of us.

After the split we were pleased when Jet enjoyed success on his own, and then with Tony Meehan, although we were a bit pissed-off at Jerry Lordan, who was a friend of all of us, for giving 'Diamonds' and 'Scarlett O'Hara' to Jet and Tony. They were great melodies and the Shadows would have loved them. Jerry told me that he felt sorry for Jet and Tony being 'sacked' and that's the reason he gave them the numbers. Tony Meehan's arrangements on those hits were brilliant.

The car crash Jet and Billie Davis suffered really finished him, and after that it seemed to be all downhill. We didn't try to help him during his bad years and there was virtually no contact on either side. We didn't even know where he was. The Shadows had moved on and we were all busy living our own lives and pursuing our careers.

Fans have commented that I don't talk about Jet a great deal. He was and still is very popular with Shadows fans. Jet is a very funny man onstage and projects a Steptoe-like persona. He takes the piss out of himself and the fans love his self-deprecating humour. They appreciate his talent, know that he has been to hell and back, identify with him and love him. What I think they sometimes forget, however, is that, in the overall history of the group, Jet was in the band for only three years and the Shadows have now been in the business for fifty years. However, I want to stress that the influence of his bass playing in those three years was absolutely enormous. Thousands of Shadows fans wanted to be like Jet Harris.

Every year I promote the *Shadowmania* event, at the Lakeside Complex, Frimley Green, near Camberley in Surrey, and Jet and Licorice Locking appear there. At these gatherings, fans often ask me if Jet and I will ever play together again as Shadows, but in all honesty I cannot see that happening. But we are friends, and I have the greatest admiration for the way he overcame his drink problem, put his life together and got back into the business.

BIBLIOGRAPHY

Books

Bronson, Fred - *The Billboard Book of Number One Hits*
  (Billboard Publications, Inc., New York) 1988
Dellar, Fred - *NME Guide to Rock Cinema*
  (Hamlyn Paperbacks, Feltham, Middx) 1981
Ellis, Royston - *The Big Beat Scene* (2nd Ed.)
  (Music Mentor Books, York) 2010
Ellis, Royston (ed.) - *The Shadows by Themselves*
  (World Distributors/Souvenir Press Consul Edition, London) 1961
Ewbank, Tim, & Stafford Hildred - *Cliff: An Intimate Portrait of a Living Legend*
  (Virgin Books, London) 2008
Gambaccini, Paul, Mike Read, Jo Rice & Tim Rice -
  The Guinness Book of British Hit Albums
  (GRRR Books Ltd/Guinness Superlatives Ltd, Enfield, Middx) 1983
Gambaccini, Paul, Tim Rice & Jonathan Rice - *British Hit Singles* (10th Ed.)
  (GRRR Publications Ltd/Guinness Publishing, Enfield, Middx) 1995
Jasper, Tony - *The Top Twenty Book*
  (Blandford, London) 1991
Nicolson, Dave - *Back On The Road Again*
  (Music Mentor Books, York) 2006
Platt, John - *London's Rock Routes*
  (Fourth Estate, London) 1985
Richard, Cliff with Penny Junor - *My Life, My Way*
  (Headline Review, London) 2008
Turner, Steve - *Cliff Richard, The Bachelor Boy*
  (Carlton Books Ltd, London) 2008
Turner, Steve - *Cliff Richard, The Biography*
  (Lion Books, Oxford) 2008
Various - *New Musical Express Annual 1963*
  (WSR Ltd, London) 1962
Wallis, Ian - *American Rock'n'Roll: The UK Tours 1956-72*
  (Music Mentor Books, York) 2003
Welch, Bruce with Howard Elson -
  Rock'n'Roll, I Gave You The Best Years Of My Life
  (Penguin Books, London) 1990
White, George R. - *35 Years of British Hit EPs*
  (Music Mentor Books, York) 2001
Whitburn, Joel - *Top Pop 1955-1982*
  (Record Research, Inc, Menomonee Falls, WI) 1983

Sleevenotes

Finnis, Rob - CD *Inside* [Rollercoaster RCCD -3010]
    (Rollercoaster Records, Chalford, Glos.) 2002

Newspapers and Magazines

Daily Express
Daily Mail
Daily Mirror
Daily Sketch
Disc
New Gandy Dancer
New Musical Express
Pipeline
Record Mirror
The Beat
The Independent

Websites

http://news.bbc.co.uk/hi/english/static/in_depth/programmes/2001/booze/jet.stm
www.btinternet.com/~shadows_archive/
www.cliffrichardsongs.com
www.grc.me.uk/ap63b.htm
www.jetharris.biz
www.jetharrisfanclub.co.uk
www.terrywebster.co.uk

UK Discography

APPENDIX I

This discography contains all of Jet's key UK releases. It excludes Cliff Richard/Shadows recordings, guest appearances, 'various artists' releases and most reissues.

45 rpm Singles

Decca F-11466	Besame Mucho Chills And Fever	1962
Decca F-11488	Main Title Theme (from 'Man With The Golden Arm') Some People	1962
Decca F-11563 *(with Tony Meehan)*	Diamonds Footstomp	1963
Decca F-11644 *(with Tony Meehan)*	Scarlet O'Hara (Doing The) Hully Gully	1963
Decca F-11710 *(with Tony Meehan)*	Applejack The Tall Texan	1963
Decca F-11841	Big Bad Bass Rifka	1964
Fontana TF-849	My Lady You Don't Live Twice	1967
SRT SRTS-75355	Theme For A Fallen Idol This Sportin' Life	1975
SRT SRTS-77389	Guitar Man Theme	1978
Q Records Q-101	Diamonds *(remake)* Big Bad Bass From Texas	1988

189

EPs

Decca DFE-8502	**JET HARRIS** Besame Mucho / Rave / Some People / Real Wild Child	1962
Decca DFE-8528 *(with Tony Meehan)*	**JET & TONY** Scarlett O'Hara / (Doing The) Hully Gully / Diamonds / Footstomp	1963

LPs

Ellie Jay EJSP-8622	**INSIDE JET HARRIS** The Stranger / *Medley:* Perfidia – Blue Moon / Sleepwalk / Dance On / Wonderful Land / F.B.I. / Spanish Harlem / Apache / Riders In The Sky / Nivram / Diamonds / Scarlett O'Hara / Shazam	1978
Q Records LPMM-1038	**ANNIVERSARY ALBUM** Diamonds / Jet Black / Besame Mucho / 36-24-36 / Big Bad Bass / Scarlett O'Hara / Applejack / Man From Nowhere / Nivram / Theme For A Fallen Idol / The Tall Texan / Again / Theme from The Man With The Golden Arm	1988

Cassette Tapes

Fan Club release *(with the Strangers)*	**LIVE IN 1985** Shazam / (Dance With The) Guitar Man / Apache / Kon-Tiki / Love Me Tender / Applejack / Wonderful Land / Scarlett O'Hara / F.B.I. / Diamonds	1990
Fan Club release	**FISTFUL OF STRINGS** 36-24-36 / Real Wild Child / In Love With The Guitar Man / Cloud Nine / Big Bad Bass From Texas / Love Me Tender / Mechanism / Walk Don't Run / The Creep / Theme For A Fallen Idol / Trilogy	1990

Fan Club release	**FISTFUL OF STRINGS II**	1996
(with the Diamonds)	Diamonds / Spanish Harlem / Ghost Riders /	
	Midnight / Time Is Tight / Tall Texan /	
	Scarlett O'Hara / Apache/ Argentina /	
	F.B.I. / Nivram / Wonderful Land	

CD Singles

Strange Country SC-0001	Back In Our Rock'n'Roll Days	1998
(with Billie Davis)	*(one-track promo single)*	
Recent & Rare Records		
RRR-1	Back In Our Rock'n'Roll Days	2003
(with Billie Davis)	*(remixed version of above)*	
Crazy Lighthouse	San Antonio	2006
CLRCD-0601	Ignition	
No label/number	No Other Baby – Live	2006
(with Billie Davis)	*(one-track single)*	

CD Albums

Q Records CDMM-1038	**ANNIVERSARY ALBUM**	1988
	Same tracks as LP.	
Castle Communications	**INSIDE**	1994
CNC-4022-2	*Reissue of 1978 LP.*	
Zing TANCD-003	**TOGETHER – THE STUDIO SESSIONS**	1994
(with Tangent)	Warm Turn (Part 1) / Stingray / F.B.I. /	
	Jet Meets General Custer '94 / Walk Don't	
	Run / Diamonds / Love Me Tender / Tres	
	Bon / Truckin' Trucker's Trot '94 / Apache /	
	Danny Boy / Warm Turn (Part 2)	
Zing ZRCD-1213	**TWO OF A KIND**	1997
(with Alan Jones)	A Shadow In Time / The Truckin' Trucker's	
	Trot / Stingray / Apache (Remix '94) /	
	Diamonds / Warm Turn / *Medley:* Sleepless	

Walk – Midnight / Jet Meets General
Custer ('94) / Walk, Don't Run / F.B.I. /
Songbird / Shazam ('94) / Apache
Wardance / A Shadow In Time (Final) /
Nivram Live *(Alan)* / Nivram Live *(Jet)*

Mustang JET-001   **THE PHOENIX RISES**   1999
Theme From Something Really Important /
Scarlett O'Hara 2000 / Last Train Home /
Beater Blocker / Simply Jerry / Dreamland /
Theme 18 / Phoenix / Spivram / Mechanism /
Here I Stand / Diamonds 2000 / Man From
Nowhere / Duane Stays Mainly On The Plane

Fan Club release   **JET HARRIS'S 60TH BIRTHDAY**   2000
(with Shadoogie   Main Title Theme (Man with the Golden
and Cliff Hall)   Arm) / 36-24-36 / Kon-Tiki / Diamonds /
Scarlett O'Hara / Theme From Something
Really Important / Gonzales / The Tall
Texan / Applejack / Man From Nowhere /
Time Is Tight / Nivram

Solent SLTD-116   **DIAMONDS ARE TRUMPS**   2002
(with Bobby Graham)   Dance With The Guitar Man / Wipe Out /
You Can't Sit Down / Diamonds / Theme
For A Fallen Idol / Time Is Tight / Man
With The Golden Arm / Gonzales / No
Other Baby / Soul Limbo / Barney's Blues /
Watermelon Man / Theme For Something
Really Important / Tequila

Fan Club release   **DIAMONDS THROUGH THE YEARS**   2003
(40 YEARS – A CELEBRATION)
Eight different versions of 'Diamonds'.

Fan Club release   **SCARLETT O'HARA**
                     THROUGH THE YEARS   2003
(40 YEARS – A CELEBRATION)
Eight different versions of 'Scarlett O'Hara'.

Rollercoaster RCCD-3010   **INSIDE**   2003
Second reissue of 1978 LP.

Crazy Lighthouse
CLRCD-0602

THE JOURNEY   2008

In The Beginning / San Antonio (Ol Skool
Mix) / It Bites / Krakatoa / The Journey /
Ignition / The 4th Man/ Hello Sid / Play It
Down / Song For Tony / Shot To Pieces /
San Antonio (Instrumental) / El Vampiro /
Diamonds

Jet's Hits

APPENDIX II

RECORD RETAILER 'TOP SINGLES' CHART

Date of chart entry	Highest position attained	Time on chart	Title	Label and catalogue number
24 May 1962	22	7 wks	**Besame Mucho** *Jet Harris*	Decca F-11466
16 Aug 1962	12	11 wks	**Main Title Theme (from 'Man With The Golden Arm')** *Jet Harris*	Decca F-11488
10 Jan 1963	1	13 wks	**Diamonds** *Jet Harris & Tony Meehan*	Decca F-11563
25 Apr 1963	2	13 wks	**Scarlet O'Hara** *Jet Harris & Tony Meehan*	Decca F-11644
5 Sep 1963	4	13 wks	**Applejack** *Jet Harris & Tony Meehan*	Decca F-11710

Chart compiled by Record Retailer, BMRB, Gallup and CIN.
Chart information courtesy of 'British Hit Singles'
by Paul Gambaccini, Jo Rice and Tim Rice
(Guinness Publishing, Enfield) 1995

NEW MUSICAL EXPRESS 'TOP SINGLES' CHART

Date of chart entry	Highest position attained	Time on chart	Title	Label and catalogue number
26 May 1962	28	1 wk	**Besame Mucho** *Jet Harris*	Decca F-11466
18 Aug 1962	15	9 wks	**Main Title Theme (from 'Man With The Golden Arm')** *Jet Harris*	Decca F-11488
8 Sep 1962	21	1 wk	**Some People** [flip of above] *Jet Harris*	Decca F-11488
12 Jan 1963	1	11 wks	**Diamonds** *Jet Harris & Tony Meehan*	Decca F-11563
27 Apr 1963	2	12 wks	**Scarlet O'Hara** *Jet Harris & Tony Meehan*	Decca F-11644
7 Sep 1963	6	9 wks	**Applejack** *Jet Harris & Tony Meehan*	Decca F-11710

Chart compiled by New Musical Express.
Chart information courtesy of '40 Years of NME Charts'
by Dafydd Rees, Barry Lazell and Roger Osborne
(Boxtree, London) 1992

MELODY MAKER 'TOP 30' CHART

Date of chart entry	Highest position attained	Time on chart	Title	Label and catalogue number
9 Jun 1962	23	3 wks	**Besame Mucho** *Jet Harris*	Decca F-11466
25 Aug 1962	11	11 wks	**Main Title Theme (from 'Man With The Golden Arm') / Some People** *Jet Harris*	Decca F-11488
12 Jan 1963	1	14 wks	**Diamonds** *Jet Harris & Tony Meehan*	Decca F-11563
27 Apr 1963	2	14 wks	**Scarlet O'Hara** *Jet Harris & Tony Meehan*	Decca F-11644
7 Sep 1963	6	11 wks	**Applejack** *Jet Harris & Tony Meehan*	Decca F-11710

Chart compiled by Melody Maker.
Chart information courtesy of
http://www.ukmix.org/forums/viewtopic.php?t=26072&postdays=0&postorder=asc&start=0

RADIO LONDON 'FAB 40' CHART

Date of chart entry	Highest position attained	Time on chart	Title	Label and catalogue number
16 Jul 1967	28	2 wks	**My Lady** *Jet Harris*	Fontana TF-849

Chart information courtesy of the Radio London Ltd website: www.radiolondon.co.uk.

RECORD RETAILER 'TOP EPs' CHART

Date of chart entry	Highest position attained	Time on chart	Title	Label and catalogue number
29 Jun 1963	3	21 wks	**JET & TONY** *Jet Harris & Tony Meehan*	Decca DFE-8528

Chart compiled by Record Retailer.
Chart information courtesy of 'British Hit EPs'
by George R. White
(Music Mentor Books, York) 2001

Index

ILLUSTRATIONS & PHOTO CREDITS

Ads on pages 49, 52 and 56 courtesy John Firminger; 79 and 82 courtesy author's collection.

Autographs on page 64 courtesy author's collection.

Back cover photo © 2011 Dave Nicolson.

Front cover photo © 2006 Dave Nicolson.

Label shots on pages 36, 48 and 54 courtesy Terry Kay.

Marriage certificate on page 30 courtesy author's collection.

Photos on pages 5 and 98 © 2011 Dave Nicolson; 18 and 41 courtesy Royston Ellis; 23, 26, 45, 50 and 55 courtesy of author's collection; 32 courtesy *Daily Mail*/Rex Features; 34 and 133 courtesy Terry Kay; 42 by Brian Lawton (courtesy Trevor Simpson); 53, 60, 157 and 171 courtesy Music Mentor Books archive; 74, 123 and 127 courtesy Margaret Harris; 80 by Steve Kramer (courtesy *The Beat* magazine); 118 and 148 courtesy Susan Meehan; 138 courtesy Laurel Jones; 167 courtesy ABC-TV/Music Mentor Books archive; 183 courtesy Bruce Welch.

Programmes on pages 20 and 39 courtesy author's collection.

Sheet music on page 37 courtesy author's collection; 47 courtesy Music Mentor Books archive.

Sleeve on page 67 courtesy Music Mentor Books archive.

INTERVIEW CREDITS

Jim Budd interview extracts courtesy of Rollercoaster Records/Rob Finnis.

Roger LaVern interview courtesy of George R. White.

Joe Moretti interview extracts courtesy of the John McLaughlin tribute website 'Son of the Pages of Fire' (www.grc.me.uk/ap63b.htm).

Other interviews conducted by author, or as credited.

OTHER TITLES FROM MUSIC MENTOR BOOKS

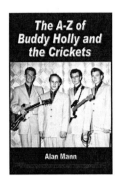

The A-Z of Buddy Holly and the Crickets
Alan Mann
ISBN-13: 978-0-9547068-0-7 *(pbk, 320 pages)* £19.99

The A-Z of Buddy Holly and the Crickets draws together a mass of Holly facts and info from a variety of published sources, as well as the author's own original research, and presents them in an easy-to-use encyclopaedic format. Now in its third edition, it has proved to be a popular and valuable reference work on this seminal rock'n'roller. It is a book that every Holly fan will want to keep at their fingertips. It is a book about a musical genius who will never be forgotten.

American Rock'n'Roll: The UK Tours 1956-72
Ian Wallis
ISBN-13: 978-0-9519888-6-2 *(pbk, 424 pages)* £19.99

The first-ever detailed overview of every visit to these shores by American (and Canadian!) rock'n'rollers. It's all here: over 400 pages of tour itineraries, support acts, show reports, TV appearances and other items of interest. Illustrated with dozens of original tour programmes, ads, ticket stubs and great live shots, many rare or previously unpublished.

Back On The Road Again
Dave Nicolson
ISBN-13: 978-0-9547068-2-1 *(pbk, 216 pages)* £12.99

A third book of interviews by Dave Nicolson in the popular *On The Road* series, this time with more of a Sixties flavour: Solomon Burke, Gene Chandler, Bruce Channel, Lowell Fulson, Jet Harris, Gene McDaniels, Scott McKenzie, Gary S. Paxton, Bobby 'Boris' Pickett, Martha Reeves & The Vandellas, Jimmie Rodgers, Gary Troxel (Fleetwoods), Leroy Van Dyke and Junior Walker.

The Big Beat Scene
Royston Ellis
ISBN-13: 978-0-9562679-1-7 *(pbk, 184 pages)* £11.99

Originally published in 1961, *The Big Beat Scene* was the first contemporary account of the teenage music scene in Britain. Written before the emergence of the Beatles, and without the benefit of hindsight, this fascinating document provides a unique, first-hand insight into the popularity and relevance of jazz, skiffle and rock'n'roll at a time when Cliff Richard & The Shadows were at the cutting edge of pop, and the social attitudes prevailing at the time.

The Chuck Berry International Directory (Volume 1)
Morten Reff
ISBN-13: 978-0-9547068-6-9 (pbk, 486 pages) £24.99

For the heavyweight Berry fan. Everything you ever wanted to know about Chuck Berry, in four enormous volumes compiled by the world-renowned Norwegian Berry collector and authority, Morten Reff. This volume contains discographies for over 40 countries, plus over 700 rare label and sleeve illustrations.

The Chuck Berry International Directory (Volume 2)
Morten Reff
ISBN-13: 978-0-9547068-7-6 (pbk, 532 pages) £24.99

The second of four volumes in this extensive reference work dedicated to rock'n'roll's most influential guitarist and composer. Contains details of bootlegs; radio albums; movies; TV shows; video and DVD releases; international tour itineraries; hits, achievements and awards; Berry's songs, roots, and influence on other artists; tributes; Chuck Berry in print; fan clubs and websites; plus annotated discographies of pianist Johnnie Johnson (post-Berry) and the ultimate Berry copyist, Eddy Clearwater.

Daynce of the Peckerwoods: The Badlands of Texas Music
Michael H. Price
ISBN-13: 978-0-9547068-5-2 (pbk, 350 pages) £18.99

From a childhood spent among such key roots-music figures as Bob Wills and Big Joe Turner, and an extended dual career as a musician and journalist, Michael H. Price has forged this frenzied chronicle of life among the denizens of the vanishing borderlands of Texas' indigenous music scene over the past half-century. Contains essays on Billy Briggs, Ornette Coleman, the Light Crust Doughboys, Big Bill Lister, Rudy Ray Moore, Eck Robertson, Ray Sharpe, Robert Shaw, Major Bill Smith, Stevie Ray Vaughan and many more.

Elvis & Buddy – Linked Lives
Alan Mann
ISBN-13: 978-0-9519888-5-5 (pbk, 160 pages) £9.99

The achievements of Elvis Presley and Buddy Holly have been extensively documented, but until now little if anything has been known about the many ways in which their lives were interconnected. The author examines each artist's early years, comparing their backgrounds and influences, chronicling all their meetings and examining the many amazing parallels in their lives, careers and tragic deaths. Over 50 photos, including many rare/previously unpublished.

The First Time We Met The Blues – A journey of discovery with Jimmy Page, Brian Jones, Mick Jagger and Keith Richards
David Williams
ISBN-13: 978-0-9547068-1-4 *(pbk, 130 pages)* £8.99

David Williams was a childhood friend of Led Zeppelin guitar legend, Jimmy Page. The author describes how they discovered the blues together, along with future members of the Rolling Stones. The climax of the book is a detailed account of a momentous journey by van from London to Manchester to see the 1962 *American Folk-Blues Festival*, where they got their first chance to see their heroes in action.

Last Swill and Testament – The hilarious, unexpurgated memoirs of
Paul 'Sailor' Vernon
ISBN-13: 978-0-9547068-4-5 *(pbk, 228 pages)* £12.99

Born in London shortly after the end of World War II, Paul 'Sailor' Vernon came into his own during the 1960s when spotty teenage herberts with bad haircuts began discovering The Blues. For the Sailor it became a lifelong obsession that led him into a whirlwind of activity as a rare record dealer, magazine proprietor/editor, video bootlegger and record company director. It's all here in this one-of-a-kind life history that will leave you reaching for an enamel bucket and a fresh bottle of disinfectant!

Let The Good Times Rock! – A Fan's Notes On Post-War American Roots Music
Bill Millar
ISBN-13: 978-0-9519888-8-6 *(pbk, 362 pages)* £18.99

For almost four decades, the name 'Bill Millar' has been synonymous with the very best in British music writing. This fabulous new book collects together 49 of his best pieces — some previously unpublished — in a thematic compilation covering hillbilly, rockabilly, R&B, rock'n'roll, doo-wop, swamp pop and soul. Includes essays on acappella, doo-wop and blue-eyed soul, as well as detailed profiles of some of the most fascinating and influential personalities of each era.

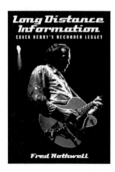

Long Distance Information: Chuck Berry's Recorded Legacy
Fred Rothwell
ISBN-13: 978-0-9519888-2-4 *(pbk, 352 pages)* £18.99

The lowdown on every recording Chuck Berry has ever made. Includes an overview of his life and career, his influences, the stories behind his most famous compositions, full session details, listings of all his key US/UK vinyl and CD releases (including track details), TV and film appearances, and much, much more. Over 100 illustrations including label shots, vintage ads and previously unpublished photos.

On The Road
Dave Nicolson
ISBN-13: 978-0-9519888-4-8 *(pbk, 256 pages)* £14.99

Gary 'US' Bonds, Pat Boone, Freddy Cannon, Crickets Jerry Allison, Sonny Curtis and Joe B. Mauldin, Bo Diddley, Dion, Fats Domino, Duane Eddy, Frankie Ford, Charlie Gracie, Brian Hyland, Marv Johnson, Ben E. King, Brenda Lee, Little Eva, Chris Montez, Johnny Moore (Drifters), Gene Pitney, Johnny Preston, Tommy Roe, Del Shannon, Edwin Starr, Johnny Tillotson and Bobby Vee tell their own fascinating stories. Over 150 illustrations including vintage ads, record sleeves, label shots, sheet music covers, etc.

On The Road Again
Dave Nicolson
ISBN-13: 978-0-9519888-9-3 *(pbk, 206 pages)* £12.99

Second volume of interviews with the stars of pop and rock'n'roll including Freddie Bell, Martin Denny, Johnny Farina (Santo & Johnny), the Kalin Twins, Robin Luke, Chas McDevitt, Phil Phillips, Marvin Rainwater, Herb Reed (Platters), Tommy Sands, Joe Terranova (Danny & The Juniors), Mitchell Torok, Marty Wilde and the 'Cool Ghoul' himself, John Zacherle.

Railroadin' Some: Railroads In The Early Blues
Max Haymes
ISBN-13: 978-0-9547068-3-8 *(pbk, 390 pages)* £18.99

This groundbreaking book, written by one of the foremost blues historians in the UK, is based on over 30 years research, exploration and absolute passion for early blues music. It is the first ever comprehensive study of the enormous impact of the railroads on 19th and early 20th Century African American society and the many and varied references to this new phenomenon in early blues lyrics. Includes ballin' the jack, smokestack lightning, hot shots, the bottoms, chain gangs, barrelhouses, hobo jungles and more.

**Music Mentor books are available from all good bookshops
or by mail order from:**

**Music Mentor Books
69 Station Road
Upper Poppleton
YORK YO26 6PZ
England**

Telephone/Fax: +44 (0)1904 330308
Email: music.mentor@lineone.net
Website: http://musicmentor0.tripod.com